100 GREAT

DESSERT

RECIPES

LADIES' HOME JOURNAL™ BOOKS
New York/Des Moines

LADIES' HOME JOURNAL™ BOOKS
An Imprint of Meredith® Books
President, Book Group: Joseph J. Ward
Vice President and Editorial Director: Elizabeth P. Rice
Art Director: Ernest Shelton

LADIES' HOME JOURNAL®
Publishing Director and Editor-in-Chief: Myrna Blyth
Food Editor: Jan Turner Hazard
Associate Food Editors: Susan Sarao Westmoreland, Lisa Brainerd

100 GREAT DESSERT RECIPES
Project Manager/Editor: Shelli McConnell
Writer/Researcher: Carol Prager
Copy Editor: Jennifer Miller
Associate Art Director: Tom Wegner
Food Stylist: Rick Ellis
Prop Stylist: Bette Blau
Photographer: Corinne Colen Photography
Production Manager: Douglas Johnston
Electronic Production Coordinator: Paula Forest

On the cover: Toffee Ice Cream Layer Cake, page 70

Meredith Corporation Corporate Officers
Chairman of the Executive Committee: E. T. Meredith III
Chairman of the Board, President and Chief Executive Officer: Jack D. Rehm
Group Presidents: Joseph J. Ward, Books; William T. Kerr, Magazines;
Philip A. Jones, Broadcasting; Allen L. Sabbag, Real Estate
Vice Presidents: Leo R. Armatis, Corporate Relations; Thomas G. Fisher, General Counsel
and Secretary; Larry D. Hartsook, Finance; Michael A. Sell, Treasurer; Kathleen J. Zehr,
Controller and Assistant Secretary

We Care!
All of us at Ladies' Home Journal™ Books are dedicated to providing you with the ideas and
recipe information you need to create wonderful foods. We welcome your comments and
suggestions. Write us at: Ladies' Home Journal™ Books, Cookbook Editorial Department,
RW-240, 1716 Locust St., Des Moines, IA 50309-3023.

If you would like to order additional copies of any of our books, call 1-800-678-2803.

To ensure that Ladies' Home Journal® recipes
meet the highest standards for flavor, nutrition,
appearance and reliability, we test them a
minimum of three times in our own kitchen.
That makes for quality you can count on.

Desserts

When it comes to desserts, nobody loves them more than
we do. For over a hundred years, desserts have been the
most popular and most-often requested of our recipes at
Ladies' Home Journal®, and we've got something for
everyone. Experience tells us that no matter what size or
form dessert takes—a towering, triple layer cake, crisp,
delicate butter cookies, totally decadent cheesecake, or a
low-fat, refreshing fruit sorbet—any time is the right time
for dessert, even when there's not a moment to spare!
So here's the ultimate collection of the sweet sensations
we all adore.

CONTENTS

Nothing But Chocolate
Decadent selections for sweet indulgences.

Serious Cookies
Big tastes delivered in small packages.

Perfect Pies, Tarts, and Cobblers
Irresistible fruit, nut, and cream fillings baked under, over, or in a crust.

Fabulous Frozen Desserts
A delectable collection of ice creams, sorbets, sherbets, and more.

NOTHING BUT

CHOCOLATE

In this collection of ultimate confections, where else can we begin but with chocolate? Dark, dense, and decadent, traditional or trendy, just dive into our Molten Chocolate Cake with warm truffle filling, Chocolate-Macadamia Nut Terrine, or satiny Old-Fashioned Chocolate Cream Pie for eternal chocolate bliss. It's our guarantee that every bite of these cocoa creations will be delectable. When we say chocolate, we mean dessert!

FALLEN CHOCOLATE SOUFFLÉ CAKE

This ultra-rich flourless cake, which boasts a full pound of chocolate, owes its light texture to fluffy beaten eggs. Completely do ahead, it's the easiest soufflé dessert you'll ever make.

Prep time: 30 minutes plus chilling
Baking time: 25 to 30 minutes
O *Degree of difficulty: easy*

8 **squares (8 ounces) semisweet chocolate, coarsely chopped**
8 **squares (8 ounces) unsweetened chocolate, coarsely chopped**
1 **cup unsalted butter, cut up (no substitutions)**
¼ **cup orange- *or* coffee-flavored liqueur**
9 **large eggs, separated, at room temperature**
¾ **cup granulated sugar**
Confectioners' sugar
Sweetened whipped cream and chocolate curls, for garnish

1 Preheat oven to 350°F. Butter the bottom of a 10-inch springform pan and line with parchment paper. Butter and flour paper and sides of pan. Melt chocolates and butter in top of double boiler over simmering water. Cool to lukewarm. Stir in liqueur.

2 Beat egg yolks and sugar in a large mixing bowl until pale and thick, and a ribbon forms when beaters are lifted. Carefully fold in chocolate mixture using a rubber spatula. Beat egg whites in a clean mixing bowl to soft peaks. Gently fold whites in three batches into chocolate mixture until blended. Pour into pan.

3 Bake 25 to 30 minutes or until cake is barely set in center. (Cake top will be cracked.) Cool on a wire rack. Cover and refrigerate cake at least 30 minutes or overnight. (If refrigerated overnight, let stand at room temperature 30 minutes before serving.) Just before serving, run a small sharp knife around edge of pan; remove sides. Sprinkle top of cake with confectioners' sugar. Serve with whipped cream and chocolate curls. Makes 20 servings.

PER SERVING		DAILY GOAL
Calories	270	2,000 (F), 2,500 (M)
Total Fat	21 g	60 g or less (F), 70 g or less (M)
Saturated fat	12 g	20 g or less (F), 23 g or less (M)
Cholesterol	121 mg	300 mg or less
Sodium	33 mg	2,400 mg or less
Carbohydrates	20 g	250 g or more
Protein	5 g	55 g to 90 g

NOTES

CHOCOLATE ANGEL FOOD CAKE

A rich chocolate cake with no fat and no cholesterol? Angel food cake is a fat-fighter's dream come true! The secret to this tender moist treat? Slowly beating the egg whites at medium, not high, speed.

Prep time: 25 minutes plus cooling
Baking time: 35 to 40 minutes
○ *Degree of difficulty: easy*

- ⅔ **cup sifted cake flour**
- ⅓ **cup unsweetened cocoa**
- 1½ **cups granulated sugar, divided**
- 12 **large egg whites, at room temperature**
- 1½ **teaspoons vanilla extract**
- 1½ **teaspoons cream of tartar**
- ½ **teaspoon salt**

1 Preheat oven to 375°F. Sift flour, cocoa, and ¾ cup of the sugar together 3 times; set aside.

2 Beat egg whites at low speed in a large mixing bowl until foamy, about 5 minutes. Add vanilla, cream of tartar, and salt.

Gradually increase speed to medium while beating in remaining ¾ cup sugar, 1 tablespoon at a time, about 5 minutes. When sugar is incorporated, continue beating to stiff peaks, 2 minutes more. Sift one-third of dry ingredients over whites; fold in with rubber spatula. Repeat process 2 more times until just blended.

3 Pour batter into an ungreased, 10-inch tube pan. Run a knife through batter to remove any large air pockets. Bake 35 to 40 minutes, or until top springs back when gently pressed with fingertip. Immediately invert pan onto neck of funnel or bottle; let hang until completely cool, about 2 hours.

4 To loosen, run a metal spatula or thin knife around side of pan and tube. Invert pan again and remove cake. Turn cake upright onto serving plate. Makes 12 servings.

PER SERVING		DAILY GOAL
Calories	140	2,000 (F), 2,500 (M)
Total Fat	0 g	60 g or less (F), 70 g or less (M)
Saturated fat	0 g	20 g or less (F), 23 g or less (M)
Cholesterol	0 mg	300 mg or less
Sodium	146 mg	2,400 mg or less
Carbohydrates	31 g	250 g or more
Protein	4 g	55 g to 90 g

MOLTEN CHOCOLATE CAKE

This sinful dessert, developed with the help of two New York chefs, Jean-Georges Vongerichten of Jo Jo and Wayne Nish owner of March, is a testament to our love affair with chocolate. In the center of these individual cakes are luscious liquefied truffles.

Ⓜ *Microwave*
Prep time: 30 minutes plus chilling
Baking time: 10 minutes
◑ *Degree of difficulty: moderate*

¼ **cup heavy *or* whipping cream**
2 **squares (2 ounces) semisweet chocolate, coarsely chopped**
4 **squares (4 ounces) semisweet chocolate, coarsely chopped**
1½ **squares (1½ ounces) unsweetened chocolate, coarsely chopped**
½ **cup plus 3 tablespoons unsalted butter (no substitutions)**
3 **large eggs, at room temperature**
3 **large egg yolks, at room temperature**
⅓ **cup granulated sugar**
⅓ **cup all-purpose flour**
1 **tablespoon confectioners' sugar Whipped cream *or* vanilla ice cream and fresh raspberries, for garnish**

1 For truffles, heat cream to boiling in a small saucepan. Remove from heat. Add the 2 ounces chopped semisweet chocolate and stir until melted and smooth; cool 10 minutes. On a sheet of wax paper, shape truffle mixture into an 8-inch log. Wrap and refrigerate 3 hours or freeze 2 hours until firm. Cut crosswise into 8 equal pieces. (Can be made ahead. Wrap and refrigerate up to 24 hours.)

2 Preheat oven to 400°F. Butter and flour eight 6-ounce custard cups; tap to remove excess flour. Place on cookie sheet.

3 For cake, melt the 4 ounces semisweet chocolate and the unsweetened chocolate and butter in a medium microwave-proof bowl on high (100% power) 2 minutes; stir until completely melted and smooth. Cool to room temperature. (Or use a double boiler over simmering water, stirring occasionally. Cool.)

4 Combine eggs, egg yolks, and sugar in a large mixing bowl. Beat at high speed until mixture is thick and a ribbon forms when beaters are lifted, 8 to 10 minutes. Sift flour over egg mixture and fold in gently with a rubber spatula. Fold in cooled chocolate-butter mixture in 2 batches, just until blended.

5 Pour batter into prepared custard cups. Bake 5 minutes. Remove from oven. With a spoon, quickly place one truffle on center of each cake (truffle will sink). Return to oven and bake 4 to 5 minutes more, or until tops of cakes are dry and begin to pull away from sides of cups. Transfer cups to a wire rack and cool 5 minutes.

6 With a small, sharp knife, carefully loosen cakes from cups and invert onto 8 dessert plates. Sift confectioners' sugar lightly over tops. Serve warm with whipped cream or ice cream and fresh raspberries. Makes 8 servings.

PER SERVING		DAILY GOAL
Calories	415	2,000 (F), 2,500 (M)
Total Fat	34 g	60 g or less (F), 70 g or less (M)
Saturated fat	19 g	20 g or less (F), 23 g or less (M)
Cholesterol	215 mg	300 mg or less
Sodium	32 mg	2,400 mg or less
Carbohydrates	27 g	250 g or more
Protein	6 g	55 g to 90 g

REINE DE SABA

The name of this rich flourless chocolate cake means "Queen of Sheba," but the origin of the cake is unknown.

Prep time: 1 hour
Baking time: 45 minutes
● *Degree of difficulty: moderate*

- 6 **ounces (1¼ cups) hazelnuts**
- ⅓ **cup plus 2 tablespoons granulated sugar**
- 9 **squares (9 ounces) semisweet chocolate, coarsely chopped, divided**
- 2 **squares (2 ounces) unsweetened chocolate, coarsely chopped**
- ½ **cup heavy *or* whipping cream**
- 1 **cup unsalted butter, softened, divided (no substitutions)**
- ⅓ **cup firmly packed dark brown sugar**
  Pinch salt
- 6 **large eggs, separated, at room temperature**
- 2 **tablespoons hazelnut-flavored liqueur**
- 1 **tablespoon water**

Mint leaves and candied violets, for garnish

1 Preheat oven to 350°F. To toast hazelnuts, bake on a baking sheet until lightly browned and skins are crackly, 12 to 15 minutes. Wrap nuts in a clean kitchen towel and let stand 5 minutes. Rub nuts in towel to remove skins; cool completely. Combine nuts and 1 tablespoon granulated sugar in food processor and pulse until mixture is finely ground.

2 For cake, heat 6 squares of the semisweet chocolate, the unsweetened chocolate, and cream in a small saucepan over low heat, stirring occasionally, until melted and smooth. Cool.

3 Butter a 9-inch springform pan. Line bottom with wax paper; butter and flour paper and tap to remove excess flour. Beat ¾ cup butter, ⅓ cup granulated sugar, the brown sugar, and salt in a large mixing bowl until light and fluffy. Beat in egg yolks, two at a time, beating well after each addition. Add cooled chocolate mixture and liqueur and beat just until blended. Stir in nut mixture.

4 Beat egg whites in a clean mixing bowl to soft peaks. Gradually beat in remaining 1 tablespoon granulated sugar and beat just until stiff. Gently fold egg whites into chocolate batter with a rubber spatula just until blended. Pour batter into prepared pan.

5 Bake 45 minutes, or until center of cake is puffed and firm. Cool on wire rack 20 minutes. Remove side of pan and invert cake onto rack. Remove bottom of pan, carefully peel off paper and cool completely.

6 For glaze, combine the remaining 3 squares semisweet chocolate, remaining ¼ cup butter, and water in a small saucepan. Heat, stirring occasionally, over low heat until chocolate is melted and glaze is smooth.

7 Pour warm glaze over cake on rack, smoothing top and sides with a thin metal spatula. Let stand at room temperature until glaze is firm, 2 hours or overnight. Garnish cake with mint leaves and candied violets. Makes 20 servings.

PER SERVING		DAILY GOAL	
Calories	290	2,000 (F), 2,500 (M)	
Total Fat	24 g	60 g or less (F), 70 g or less (M)	
Saturated fat	11 g	20 g or less (F), 23 g or less (M)	
Cholesterol	97 mg	300 mg or less	
Sodium	34 mg	2,400 mg or less	
Carbohydrates	19 g	250 g or more	
Protein	4 g	55 g to 90 g	

ONE-BOWL CHOCOLATE CUPCAKES

These frosted cupcakes are perfect for birthdays and bake sales. And nothing could be simpler—just pour the liquid ingredients into the dry ones, stir, and bake.

Prep time: 30 minutes plus cooling
Baking time: 15 to 18 minutes
○ *Degree of difficulty: easy*

- 1½ **cups milk**
- 1 **teaspoon white vinegar**
- 1¾ **cups all-purpose flour**
- 1½ **cups granulated sugar**
- ⅔ **cup unsweetened cocoa**
- 1 **teaspoon baking powder**
- ½ **teaspoon baking soda**
- ¼ **teaspoon salt**
- ¾ **cup butter *or* margarine, softened, cut up**
- 2 **large eggs**
- 1 **teaspoon vanilla extract**

Fluffy White Frosting
- 1 **large egg white**
- ½ **cup granulated sugar**
- 2 **tablespoons water**
- 1 **tablespoon light corn syrup**
- ⅛ **teaspoon cream of tartar**
- ½ **teaspoon vanilla extract**
  Unsweetened cocoa, for garnish

1 Preheat oven to 350°F. Line 24 muffin-pan cups with paper liners. Combine milk and vinegar in a 2-cup glass measure. Let stand 5 minutes.

2 Combine flour, sugar, cocoa, baking powder, baking soda, and salt in a large mixing bowl. At low speed, beat in butter until mixture is crumbly. Add milk-vinegar mixture, eggs, and vanilla then beat at medium speed for 3 minutes until smooth. Spoon about ¼ cup batter into each paper liner.

3 Bake 15 to 18 minutes or until top springs back when gently pressed with fingertip. Cool in pan on wire rack 5 minutes, then remove cupcakes from pan to cool completely. Spread tops with warm Fluffy White Frosting and sprinkle lightly with cocoa. Makes 2 dozen.

Fluffy White Frosting: Combine egg white, sugar, water, corn syrup, and cream of tartar in top of a double boiler over rapidly boiling water. Beat constantly with a hand-held mixer until thick and fluffy, 3 to 4 minutes. Remove from heat, add vanilla and beat until stiff enough to spread.

One-Bowl Sheet Cake: Prepare batter as at left. Grease a 13x9-inch baking pan. Line bottom with wax paper, grease and flour paper and sides. Pour batter into prepared pan. Bake 30 to 35 minutes or until top springs back when gently pressed with fingertip. Cool in pan on wire rack 10 minutes. Invert cake onto rack; remove paper and cool completely. Frost cake with warm Fluffy White Frosting and sprinkle lightly with cocoa. Makes 24 servings.

PER CUPCAKE OR PIECE		DAILY GOAL
Calories	175	2,000 (F), 2,500 (M)
Total Fat	7 g	60 g or less (F), 70 g or less (M)
Saturated fat	4 g	20 g or less (F), 23 g or less (M)
Cholesterol	35 mg	300 mg or less
Sodium	132 mg	2,400 mg or less
Carbohydrates	26 g	250 g or more
Protein	3 g	55 g to 90 g

CLASSIC SACHER TORTE

One of Europe's most famous desserts, this cake is truly a testimonial to Viennese pastry and chocolate.

Prep time: 40 minutes plus cooling
Baking time: 45 minutes
Degree of difficulty: moderate

- 5 **squares (5 ounces) semisweet chocolate, coarsely chopped**
- ½ **cup butter, softened (no substitutions)**
- 1 **cup confectioners' sugar, sifted and divided**
- 4 **large eggs, separated**
- 1 **teaspoon vanilla extract**
- ¼ **teaspoon salt**
- ⅓ **cup cake flour, sifted**
- ¾ **cup finely ground almonds**
- ⅓ **cup apricot preserves**
- 3 **tablespoons light corn syrup**
- 3 **tablespoons water**
- 2 **tablespoons butter (no substitutions)**
- 6 **squares (6 ounces) semisweet chocolate, coarsely chopped**
  Sweetened whipped cream

1 Preheat oven to 350°F. Grease and flour a 9-inch springform pan. Melt chocolate in top of double boiler over simmering water. Cool. Beat butter in a large mixing bowl until creamy. Gradually beat in ½ cup of the confectioners' sugar. Beat in egg yolks, one at a time, beating well after each addition. Beat in melted chocolate, vanilla, and salt, to blend.

2 Beat egg whites in a clean mixing bowl until foamy. Gradually beat in remaining ½ cup confectioners' sugar and continue to beat until stiff but not dry. Gently fold whites in three batches into chocolate mixture with a rubber spatula. Fold in flour, then almonds, just until blended. Spread evenly in the prepared pan.

3 Bake 45 minutes or until toothpick inserted in center comes out clean. Cool on wire rack 10 minutes, then remove sides of pan. Invert cake onto another rack and cool completely.

4 With a long serrated knife, cut cake into 2 layers. Place top layer cut side up on a serving plate. Arrange strips of wax paper underneath edges of cake to catch any drips from glaze.

5 Heat preserves in a small saucepan over low heat; spread on cut side of cake layer. Top with remaining layer cut side down.

6 For glaze, bring syrup, water, and butter to a boil in a medium saucepan. Remove from heat. Add chocolate and whisk until melted and smooth. Reserve 3 tablespoons of glaze. Pour remaining glaze on cake; spreading on top and sides with a metal spatula. Let stand 1 hour or until glaze sets.

7 Spoon reserved glaze into a small pastry bag fitted with a #2 plain tip. Pipe "Sacher" on top of cake. Remove wax paper strips. Serve with sweetened whipped cream. Makes 12 servings.

PER SERVING		DAILY GOAL
Calories	360	2,000 (F), 2,500 (M)
Total Fat	22 g	60 g or less (F), 70 g or less (M)
Saturated fat	12 g	20 g or less (F), 23 g or less (M)
Cholesterol	98 mg	300 mg or less
Sodium	180 mg	2,400 mg or less
Carbohydrates	40 g	250 g or more
Protein	5 g	55 g to 90 g

BIG AND BEAUTIFUL BROWNIES

It's hard to believe that before the 1920s, brownies were made without chocolate. Adding that glorious ingredient makes this rich bar cookie a great American dessert. You'll love this extra-thick, fudgy version.

Prep time: 10 minutes
Baking time: 30 to 32 minutes
○ *Degree of difficulty: easy*

- ¾ **cup all-purpose flour**
- ¾ **cup unsweetened cocoa**
- ¼ **teaspoon salt**
- ¾ **cup butter *or* margarine, melted**
- 1 **teaspoon instant coffee powder**
- 1½ **cups granulated sugar**
- 3 **large eggs**
- 1½ **teaspoons vanilla extract**
- ½ **pound walnuts, toasted and coarsely chopped**

1 Preheat oven to 350°F. Grease a 9-inch square baking pan. Combine flour, cocoa, and salt in a medium bowl.

2 Whisk butter and coffee powder together in a large bowl. Add sugar, whisking to blend. Add eggs, one at a time, beating well after each addition. Whisk in vanilla. Whisk in dry ingredients just until blended. Stir in nuts.

3 Pour batter into prepared pan. Bake 30 to 32 minutes or until toothpick inserted in center comes out barely clean. Cool in pan on wire rack. Cut into 16 squares.

PER SERVING		DAILY GOAL
Calories	290	2,000 (F), 2,500 (M)
Total Fat	19 g	60 g or less (F), 70 g or less (M)
Saturated fat	7 g	20 g or less (F), 23 g or less (M)
Cholesterol	63 mg	300 mg or less
Sodium	135 mg	2,400 mg or less
Carbohydrates	28 g	250 g or more
Protein	5 g	55 g to 90 g

THE TASTE OF CHOCOLATE

Chocolate is simply sublime when eaten out of hand. Here's what to look for in the best chocolate.

Appearance: The color of chocolate can range from light to dark. It can be shiny, have an even surface, or a streaky appearance. Sometimes you'll see a sugar "bloom," a white mottling which does not affect the flavor of the chocolate.

Aroma: This can vary greatly. It can be nutty, perfumed, cherry, fruity, toasted, burnt, musty, earthy, or floral.

Mouth feel and texture: When you break a piece of chocolate, look for a clean, even break. Chocolate may also be crisp, soft, dry, crumbly, smooth, grainy, waxy, or chalky. Chocolate that is rich in cocoa butter literally melts in your mouth (the melting point of cocoa butter is 92°F.).

Taste: All the words that describe aroma can apply to taste. Consider also, winey, tannic, coffeelike, acidic, metallic, nutty, vanilla, soapy, sweet, and medicinal.

WARM BROWNIE PUDDING

As this one-bowl cake bakes, a gooey fudge pudding forms on the bottom of the pan and a moist double chocolate brownie cake rises to the top like magic.

Prep time: 15 minutes
Baking time: 35 minutes
○ *Degree of difficulty: easy*

1   **cup all-purpose flour**
½   **cup granulated sugar**
½   **cup unsweetened cocoa, divided**
2   **teaspoons baking powder**
¼   **teaspoon salt**
½   **cup milk**
2   **tablespoons butter *or* margarine, melted**
1   **teaspoon vanilla extract**
½   **cup semisweet chocolate chips**
½   **cup firmly packed brown sugar**
1¾ **cups boiling water**
    Vanilla *or* peppermint ice cream

1 Preheat oven to 350°F. Combine flour, granulated sugar, ¼ cup of the cocoa, baking powder, and salt in a large bowl. Stir in milk, butter, and vanilla until smooth; stir in chocolate chips. Spread evenly in bottom of an ungreased, shallow 1½-quart casserole.

2 Sprinkle brown sugar and remaining ¼ cup cocoa on top. Place casserole in oven; carefully pour boiling water over the top. Bake 35 minutes or until top springs back when gently pressed with fingertip. Cool 10 minutes before serving. Serve warm with ice cream. Makes 6 servings.

PER SERVING (WITHOUT ICE CREAM)		DAILY GOAL
Calories	350	2,000 (F), 2,500 (M)
Total Fat	11 g	60 g or less (F), 70 g or less (M)
Saturated fat	6 g	20 g or less (F), 23 g or less (M)
Cholesterol	13 mg	300 mg or less
Sodium	288 mg	2,400 mg or less
Carbohydrates	63 g	250 g or more
Protein	5 g	55 g to 90 g

17

HAZELNUT-TRUFFLE CHEESECAKE

Totally indulgent but worth it! Each bite packs such fabulous flavor that even the most die-hard chocoholics won't feel cheated.

Prep time: 50 minutes plus chilling
Baking time: 65 minutes
Degree of difficulty: moderate

½ **cup hazelnuts, toasted and skinned (see tip, page 122)**
2 **tablespoons sugar**
½ **cup all-purpose flour**
   Pinch salt
¼ **cup cold unsalted butter, cut up (no substitutions)**
3 **packages (8 ounces each) cream cheese *or* Neufchâtel cheese, at room temperature**
1¼ **cups sugar**
12 **squares (12 ounces) bittersweet *or* semisweet chocolate, melted and cooled**
2 **teaspoons vanilla extract**
4 **large eggs, at room temperature**

¾ **cup heavy *or* whipping cream**
2 **tablespoons unsweetened cocoa**
2 **squares (2 ounces) bittersweet *or* semisweet chocolate, melted**
20 **whole hazelnuts, toasted and skinned**

1 Preheat oven to 350°F. For crust, butter a 9-inch springform pan. In a food processor, process nuts and 2 tablespoons of the sugar until ground fine. Add flour and salt, pulse to blend. Add butter and pulse until mixture resembles fine crumbs and just begins to hold together. Pat crumbs evenly over bottom of prepared pan. Bake 20 to 25 minutes or until top is golden. Cool on wire rack. Keep oven on. Tightly cover bottom and outsides of springform pan with heavy-duty foil.

2 Meanwhile, for filling, beat cream cheese in large mixing bowl at medium-high speed until light and fluffy, 2 minutes. Gradually beat in the remaining 1¼ cups sugar, scraping sides of bowl with a rubber spatula, until mixture is completely smooth, 3 minutes. Reduce speed to medium. Beat in the 12 squares melted chocolate, vanilla, and a pinch of salt. Add eggs, one at a time, beating just until

blended after each addition. Add cream, then cocoa and beat just until batter is blended.

3 Pour filling over crust in pan and place in a large roasting pan. Place pan on oven rack. Carefully pour enough hot water into roasting pan to come 1 inch up side of springform pan. Bake 60 to 65 minutes or until center is just set.

4 Remove cheesecake from water. Cool completely on wire rack. Remove foil. Cover and refrigerate overnight.

5 Just before serving, run a small sharp knife around edge of pan; remove sides. Dip each whole hazelnut halfway into the 2 squares melted chocolate and arrange decoratively around edge of cake. Drizzle or pipe remaining chocolate over cake. Makes 20 servings.

PER SERVING		DAILY GOAL
Calories	365	2,000 (F), 2,500 (M)
Total Fat	28 g	60 g or less (F), 70 g or less (M)
Saturated fat	16 g	20 g or less (F), 23 g or less (M)
Cholesterol	99 mg	300 mg or less
Sodium	131 mg	2,400 mg or less
Carbohydrates	27 g	250 g or more
Protein	6 g	55 g to 90 g

RICH CHOCOLATE TART WITH CAPPUCCINO SAUCE

This sophisticated tart features a satiny chocolate filling baked in a flaky pastry crust. The secret to the robust cappuccino custard sauce is freshly ground espresso coffee beans.

Prep time: 35 minutes plus chilling
Baking time: 35 minutes
Degree of difficulty: moderate

- 1 **cup all-purpose flour**
- 3 **tablespoons granulated sugar**
- ¼ **teaspoon salt**
- ½ **cup cold, unsalted butter, cut up (no substitutions)**
- ½ **cup unsalted butter (no substitutions)**
- 4 **squares (4 ounces) semisweet chocolate, coarsely chopped**
- 2 **squares (2 ounces) unsweetened chocolate, coarsely chopped**
- ½ **cup granulated sugar**
- ½ **cup heavy *or* whipping cream**
- 1 **teaspoon vanilla extract**
- 3 **large eggs, lightly beaten**

Cappuccino Sauce
- 2 **cups milk**
- 1 **to 2 tablespoons coarsely ground espresso coffee beans (do not use instant powder)**
- 1 **cinnamon stick**
- 4 **large egg yolks**
- ⅓ **cup granulated sugar**

1 Preheat oven to 400°F. Combine flour, the 3 tablespoons sugar, and salt in a food processor; pulse to blend. Add ½ cup cold butter and process, pulsing, until dough begins to hold together. Gather dough gently and shape into a ball. Roll into a 10-inch circle between 2 sheets of lightly floured wax paper. Refrigerate 5 minutes. Remove top sheet of wax paper and fit pastry, wax paper side up, into a 9-inch tart pan with removable bottom. Freeze 1 hour.

2 Remove remaining wax paper and place pastry on a cookie sheet. Bake 15 minutes or until golden. Cool completely on a rack.

3 Reduce oven heat to 350°F. Melt the ½ cup butter with semisweet and unsweetened chocolates in a double boiler over simmering water. Remove from heat and stir in ½ cup sugar, cream, and vanilla, then eggs until smooth. Pour into cooled tart shell and place on a cookie sheet. Bake 20 minutes or until filling is just set. Carefully remove sides of pan and cool completely on wire rack. Serve with Cappuccino Sauce. Makes 8 servings.

Cappuccino Sauce: Bring milk to a boil in a medium saucepan. Remove from heat and stir in coffee and cinnamon. Let stand 20 to 30 minutes to allow flavors to blend. Strain coffee mixture through a fine sieve lined with cheesecloth into a clean saucepan and reheat over medium heat. Meanwhile, whisk egg yolks with sugar in a small bowl. Gradually whisk in hot milk; add to pan and cook over medium-low heat, stirring constantly, just until mixture is thickened and coats back of a spoon *(do not boil)*. Strain again through a sieve into a clean bowl. Cover surface with plastic wrap and refrigerate at least 2 hours. (Can be made ahead. Refrigerate up to 4 hours.) Makes 1½ cups.

PER SERVING WITH 2 TABLESPOONS SAUCE		DAILY GOAL
Calories	655	2,000 (F), 2,500 (M)
Total Fat	46 g	60 g or less (F), 70 g or less (M)
Saturated fat	26 g	20 g or less (F), 23 g or less (M)
Cholesterol	240 mg	300 mg or less
Sodium	129 mg	2,400 mg or less
Carbohydrates	56 g	250 g or more
Protein	8 g	55 g to 90 g

OLD-FASHIONED CHOCOLATE CREAM PIE

This dessert is a true nostalgia trip. A dark chocolate pudding nestles in a crisp crust and is topped with sweet whipped cream.

Prep time: 20 minutes plus chilling
Degree of difficulty: easy

1 **cup granulated sugar**
¼ **cup cornstarch**
¼ **teaspoon salt**
2¾ **cups milk**
3 **large egg yolks**
3 **squares (3 ounces) unsweetened chocolate, coarsely chopped**
1 **tablespoon butter *or* margarine**
1 **teaspoon vanilla extract**
1 **single 9-inch baked pastry crust**
1 **cup heavy *or* whipping cream**
2 **tablespoons granulated sugar**

1 For filling, combine sugar, cornstarch, and salt in a large saucepan. Gradually whisk in milk until smooth. Bring to boil over medium-high heat, stirring gently; boil 1 minute. Remove from heat.

2 Beat egg yolks lightly in a small bowl. Gradually whisk in 1 cup hot filling, then return to saucepan, whisking constantly. Return to boil and boil 1 minute more. Remove from heat; whisk in chocolate, butter, and vanilla until completely smooth. Pour filling into baked pastry crust. Cool 15 minutes on a wire rack. Cover surface of filling with wax paper or plastic wrap and refrigerate at least 3 hours.

3 Just before serving, in a large chilled mixing bowl, beat heavy cream and confectioners' sugar until soft peaks form. Remove paper from filling and spread whipped cream over pie. Makes 8 servings.

PER SERVING		DAILY GOAL
Calories	480	2,000 (F), 2,500 (M)
Total Fat	30 g	60 g or less (F), 70 g or less (M)
Saturated fat	15 g	20 g or less (F), 23 g or less (M)
Cholesterol	136 mg	300 mg or less
Sodium	275 mg	2,400 mg or less
Carbohydrates	50 g	250 g or more
Protein	7 g	55 g to 90 g

CHOCOLATE-MACADAMIA NUT TERRINE

With five layers of bittersweet and milk chocolate ganache, this is one of the richest, most elegant desserts we created! *Pictured on page 6.*

Prep time: 1½ hours
⬤ *Degree of difficulty: moderate*

Praline
¼ **cup granulated sugar**
¼ **cup macadamia nuts, toasted and chopped**
¼ **cup blanched almonds, toasted and chopped**

Bittersweet Chocolate Ganache
½ **cup heavy *or* whipping cream**
3 **bars (3 ounces each) bittersweet chocolate**
1½ **tablespoons cognac *or* brandy**

Milk-Chocolate Ganache
⅓ **cup heavy *or* whipping cream**
3 **bars (3 ounces each) milk chocolate**
1½ **tablespoons coffee-flavored liqueur**

Glaze
½ **bar (1½ ounces) bittersweet chocolate**
1½ **tablespoons unsalted butter, cut up (no substitutions)**
1½ **teaspoons cognac**
1 **teaspoon light corn syrup**
1 **tablespoon sifted unsweetened cocoa, for garnish**

Crème Anglaise
2 **large egg yolks**
2 **tablespoons sugar**
  Pinch salt
1 **cup half-and-half cream**
1½ **teaspoons vanilla extract**

1 For praline, lightly oil a cookie sheet. Heat sugar in a small, heavy skillet over medium heat, swirling pan, until sugar is melted and forms an amber syrup, about 10 minutes (*do not stir*). Stir in nuts and spread on prepared cookie sheet. Cool. Break praline into small pieces and process in food processor until nuts are chopped fine. (Can be made ahead. Store in an airtight container at room temperature up to 24 hours.)

2 For bittersweet ganache, heat cream to scalding in a small saucepan. Process chocolate in food processor until chopped fine. With machine on, pour hot cream through feed tube in a thin, steady stream. Process until smooth, 10 seconds. Add cognac and process 1 second more. Transfer to a medium bowl and cool at room temperature until firm enough to hold its shape, about 1 hour.

3 For milk chocolate ganache, in clean food processor bowl, repeat procedure for bittersweet ganache, but substitute milk chocolate for bittersweet chocolate and coffee-flavored liqueur for cognac.

4 Line a 3 cup, 7½x3½-inch loaf pan with plastic wrap. Fill a pastry bag fitted with a ¼-inch plain tip with bittersweet ganache. Fill another pastry bag fitted with a ½-inch plain tip with milk chocolate ganache. Pipe one-third of bittersweet ganache into lines about ⅛ inch apart lengthwise along bottom of prepared loaf pan. With a small spatula, smooth chocolate evenly over bottom of pan. Sprinkle one-fourth of praline over chocolate. Repeat procedure for next layer, using half the milk chocolate ganache, topping with one-fourth of praline. Continue with another layer of bittersweet, then remaining milk chocolate, finishing with remaining bittersweet. (There should be three bittersweet and two milk chocolate layers.) Cover and refrigerate overnight or up to one week.

4 For glaze, heat all ingredients in top of double boiler over simmering water until chocolate is melted. Remove from heat and stir until smooth. Cool until slightly thickened, 10 minutes.

5 Remove terrine from refrigerator. Invert onto wire rack placed on cookie sheet, lift off loaf pan and peel off plastic wrap. Pour warm glaze over terrine, smoothing top and sides with a thin metal spatula. Refrigerate until glaze is set, 10 minutes. Sprinkle top and sides with cocoa; serve with Crème Anglaise. Makes 16 servings.

Crème Anglaise: Whisk yolks, sugar, and salt in a medium bowl until thick and pale yellow. Heat cream to scalding in heavy saucepan. Slowly pour hot cream into egg mixture in a thin, steady stream, whisking constantly. Return mixture to pan and cook, stirring, over low heat until thick enough to coat the back of a spoon, 5 to 7 minutes. Remove from heat and stir in vanilla. Strain custard through a fine sieve into a medium bowl; refrigerate until chilled. (Can be made ahead. Cover and refrigerate up to 24 hours.)

PER SERVING		DAILY GOAL
Calories	305	2,000 (F), 2,500 (M)
Total Fat	23 g	60 g or less (F), 70 g or less (M)
Saturated fat	11 g	20 g or less (F), 23 g or less (M)
Cholesterol	55 mg	300 mg or less
Sodium	36 mg	2,400 mg or less
Carbohydrates	25 g	250 g or more
Protein	4 g	55 g to 90 g

A DICTIONARY OF CHOCOLATE

Here's a glossary of terms for all chocoholics and chocolate connoisseurs:

Chocolate liquor is the base substance of all real chocolate and cocoa products. It comes from ground nibs, which are the core of cocoa beans.

Unsweetened chocolate (or baking or cooking chocolate) is chocolate liquor that has been cooled and molded.

Semisweet chocolate, or dark chocolate, is a blend of chocolate liquor, sugar, and cocoa butter, a vegetable fat extracted from chocolate liquor. It's available in bars, squares, and baking chips.

Sweet chocolate is a combination of chocolate liquor, sugar, vanilla, and cocoa butter. It contains more sugar than does semisweet chocolate. It usually comes in bars and is good for baking and eating.

Bittersweet chocolate is a sub-category of sweet chocolate. It contains chocolate liquor, milk, extra cocoa butter (to make it melt easily for baking), and sugar.

Unsweetened cocoa is what remains after the cocoa butter has been removed from the chocolate liquor. Naturally low in fat and sodium, it has no additives or preservatives.

Milk chocolate, the most common type, contains chocolate liquor, cocoa butter, milk or cream, sugar, and flavorings. Milk chocolate must contain at least 10 percent chocolate liquor.

White chocolate is not strictly a chocolate because it contains no chocolate liquor, which is what gives chocolate its color and flavor. Currently there are no federal standards for white chocolate. It may be made with vegetable fats, colorings, and flavorings.

SERIOUS

COOKIES

Here's proof that the best things come in small packages! Sweetly sophisticated and irresistibly delicious, this special assortment of miniature Lemon Meringue Tartlets, quick puff pastry Palmiers, Raspberry-Hazelnut Brownies, and Cherry Almond Pinwheels aren't just for kids. Definitely a centerpiece attraction and just as easy as they are beautiful, you won't need a cookie jar for these delicious finger treats.

LEMON MERINGUE TARTLETS

This elegant cookie is a bite-size version of one of our all-time favorite desserts.

Prep time: 45 minutes plus chilling
Baking time: 20 minutes
⬤ *Degree of difficulty: moderate*

- **1 teaspoon grated lemon peel**
- **½ cup fresh lemon juice**
- **½ cup granulated sugar**
- **½ cup unsalted butter, chilled, divided (no substitutions)**
- **4 large egg yolks**
- **1¼ cups all-purpose flour**
- **Pinch salt**
- **2 tablespoons vegetable shortening**
- **3 to 4 tablespoons ice water**
- **2 large egg whites, at room temperature**
- **⅓ cup granulated sugar**

1 For filling, combine lemon peel, lemon juice, the ½ cup sugar, and ¼ cup of the butter in a small saucepan. Bring to a boil; stir, over medium heat and boil 1 minute. Remove from heat. Whisk egg yolks in a small bowl. Slowly whisk one-fourth of the hot lemon mixture into the yolks. Add yolk mixture to saucepan, then whisk over low heat until thickened, 2 to 3 minutes (do not boil). Pour filling into a clean bowl. Cover and refrigerate until cold.

2 Preheat oven to 375°F. For tart shells, combine flour and salt in a medium bowl. Cut in the remaining ¼ cup butter and shortening with pastry blender or 2 knives until mixture resembles coarse crumbs. Add water 1 tablespoon at a time, tossing with a fork until pastry comes together. Shape into 2 thick disks. Wrap in plastic wrap and refrigerate 20 minutes.

3 Place 2-inch round tartlet pans on a cookie sheet. On a lightly floured surface, roll half the pastry into an 11x8-inch rectangle. Fit into pans. Trim excess; prick with a fork. Repeat process with remaining pastry; re-rolling scraps. Line pans with foil. Bake 12 minutes or until pastry is golden. Transfer tartlet pans to wire rack; cool in pans. Unmold tart shells, then spoon 1½ teaspoons lemon filling into each.

4 Preheat oven to 400° F. For meringue, beat egg whites in a small mixing bowl at medium speed until foamy. Gradually beat in the ⅓ cup sugar, one tablespoon at a time. Gradually increase speed to high, beating to stiff peaks. Spoon meringue into a pastry bag fitted with a ¼-inch star tip. Pipe swirls of meringue over lemon filling. Bake tartlets 5 minutes or until meringue is golden. Transfer to wire racks to cool. Makes 28.

PER TARTLET		DAILY GOAL	
Calories	95	2,000 (F), 2,500 (M)	
Total Fat	5 g	60 g or less (F), 70 g or less (M)	
Saturated fat	2 g	20 g or less (F), 23 g or less (M)	
Cholesterol	39 mg	300 mg or less	
Sodium	29 mg	2,400 mg or less	
Carbohydrates	12 g	250 g or more	
Protein	1 g	55 g to 90 g	

NOTES

_____

_____

_____

_____

_____

_____

MADELEINES

These delicate orange sponge cookies, baked in a special scalloped mold, are not too sweet and are simply perfect with coffee or tea.

Prep time: 20 minutes
Baking time: 10 to 12 minutes
○ *Degree of difficulty: easy*

½ **cup plus 2 tablespoons butter, melted (no substitutions)**
2 **large eggs**
½ **cup granulated sugar**
1 **teaspoon vanilla extract**
½ **teaspoon grated orange peel**
¼ **teaspoon salt**
¾ **cup all-purpose flour**
   Confectioners' sugar

1 Preheat oven to 350°F. Brush 24 madeleine molds with 2 tablespoons of the butter. Flour molds, tapping out excess. Beat eggs, granulated sugar, vanilla, orange peel, and salt in a mixer bowl until thick and lemon colored, 3 minutes. With a rubber spatula fold in flour, alternating with the remaining ½ cup butter, beginning and ending with flour.

2 Fill molds three-fourths full. Bake 10 to 12 minutes, until edges are golden and pull away from molds. Unmold onto wire racks to cool. When cool, sift confectioners' sugar over scalloped side. Makes 2 dozen.

PER COOKIE		DAILY GOAL
Calories	80	2,000 (F), 2,500 (M)
Total Fat	5 g	60 g or less (F), 70 g or less (M)
Saturated fat	3 g	20 g or less (F), 23 g or less (M)
Cholesterol	31 mg	300 mg or less
Sodium	77 mg	2,400 mg or less
Carbohydrates	8 g	250 g or more
Protein	1 g	55 g to 90 g

MEASURE FOR MEASURE

Use nesting metal cups and measuring spoons to measure flour and other dry ingredients. Before measuring, stir the flour in its canister or package to aerate, then spoon it into the appropriate size measuring cup. Level off any excess with a metal spatula.

Measure liquids in clear measuring cups with spouts and hold the cup at eye level for accuracy.

PECAN DIAMONDS

This totally indulgent praline bar cookie, with a buttery shortbread crust and taffy-like topping, has been a Ladies' Home Journal Test Kitchen favorite for many years. *Also pictured on page 24.*

Prep time: 20 minutes plus cooling
Baking time: 45 minutes
Degree of difficulty: moderate

- **2 cups all-purpose flour**
- **½ cup granulated sugar**
- **½ teaspoon baking powder**
- **¼ teaspoon salt**
- **¾ cup butter, chilled, divided (no substitutions)**
- **2 large eggs, lightly beaten**
- **⅔ cup light corn syrup**
- **1⅓ cups packed light brown sugar**
- **½ cup heavy *or* whipping cream**
- **1 tablespoon dark rum**
- **1 teaspoon instant coffee powder**
- **2 teaspoons vanilla extract**
- **4 cups pecan halves, toasted**

1 Preheat oven to 350°F. Line a 15½x10½-inch jelly-roll pan with foil. Coat with vegetable cooking spray. Combine flour, granulated sugar, baking powder, and salt in a medium bowl. Cut in ½ cup of the butter with a pastry blender or 2 knives until mixture resembles coarse crumbs. Stir in eggs with a fork just until pastry holds together. Transfer to a floured surface and knead lightly then pat along bottom of prepared pan. Bake 15 minutes. Cool on wire rack.

2 Meanwhile, combine corn syrup and brown sugar in a medium saucepan. Bring to boil, stirring occasionally, over medium heat. Stir in the remaining ¼ cup butter and cream; return to a boil. Reduce heat; simmer, stirring occasionally, 3 minutes. Remove from heat. Stir in rum, coffee, vanilla, and pecans. Pour evenly over pastry. Bake 30 minutes, rotating pan twice. Cool.

3 Invert pan onto cutting board; remove pan and carefully peel off foil. Invert pastry again and cut into 1-inch diamonds. Makes 12 dozen.

PER BAR		DAILY GOAL
Calories	55	2,000 (F), 2,500 (M)
Total Fat	3 g	60 g or less (F), 70 g or less (M)
Saturated fat	1 g	20 g or less (F), 23 g or less (M)
Cholesterol	7 mg	300 mg or less
Sodium	19 mg	2,400 mg or less
Carbohydrates	6 g	250 g or more
Protein	0 g	55 g to 90 g

NOTES

_____

_____

_____

_____

_____

_____

_____

_____

STORING COOKIES

Most cookies can be stored at room temperature for a few days without losing their freshly baked flavor. For longer storage, they should be frozen. Cool completely, then place cookies between sheets of wax paper in airtight, freezer-proof containers. Freeze up to 3 months. Thaw covered at room temperature about 2 hours. To thaw only some of the cookies, place them in a single layer on a serving plate for 15 minutes.

APRICOT-ALMOND STREUSEL BARS

These crumb-topped bars feature toasted almonds and a buttery shortbread crust. Try your favorite fruit preserves in the filling.

Prep time: 30 minutes plus cooling
Baking time: 50 minutes
O *Degree of difficulty: easy*

- 3½ **cups all-purpose flour, divided**
- 1 **teaspoon salt, divided**
- 1½ **cups butter *or* margarine, softened, divided**
- ¾ **cup confectioners' sugar**
- 1 **teaspoon vanilla extract**
- 1 **jar (12 ounces) apricot preserves**
- 1½ **teaspoons baking powder**
- ⅔ **cup granulated sugar**
- ⅔ **cup firmly packed brown sugar**
- ¼ **teaspoon almond extract**
- 3 **large eggs**
- 1 **cup chopped almonds, toasted**

1 Preheat oven to 350°F. Grease a 15½x10½-inch jelly-roll pan. Combine 2 cups of the flour and ½ teapoon of the salt in a medium bowl. Beat ¾ cup of the butter, confectioners' sugar, and vanilla in a large mixing bowl on medium speed until light and fluffy. With mixer at low speed, gradually add dry ingredients, beating until well combined (dough will be crumbly).

2 Press dough evenly into prepared pan. Bake 20 minutes or until golden. Cool on wire rack 5 minutes, then spread preserves over warm crust. Cool completely.

3 For topping, combine remaining 1½ cups flour, baking powder, and remaining ½ teaspoon salt in a medium bowl. Beat the remaining ¾ cup butter, granulated sugar, brown sugar, and almond extract in a large mixing bowl on medium speed until light and fluffy. Add eggs, 1 at a time, beating well after each addition. Stir in chopped almonds. Spread topping evenly over crust. Bake 30 minutes. Cool completely on wire rack. Cut into 2x1-inch bars. Makes 6 dozen.

PER BAR		DAILY GOAL
Calories	105	2,000 (F), 2,500 (M)
Total Fat	5 g	60 g or less (F), 70 g or less (M)
Saturated fat	3 g	20 g or less (F), 23 g or less (M)
Cholesterol	19 mg	300 mg or less
Sodium	85 mg	2,400 mg or less
Carbohydrates	13 g	250 g or more
Protein	1 g	55 g to 90 g

NOTES

CHOCOLATE BUTTONS

These delicate morsels of fudgy chocolate get their luscious flavor from toasted hazelnuts.

Prep time: 40 minutes
Baking time: 5 to 8 minutes per batch
Degree of difficulty: moderate

- 1 **cup hazelnuts, toasted, skinned and minced (see tip, page 122)**
- 6 **tablespoons all-purpose flour**
- 6 **tablespoons unsweetened cocoa**
- ⅛ **teaspoon ground cloves (optional)**
  Pinch salt
- ½ **cup butter *or* margarine, softened**
- ½ **cup plus 2 tablespoons sugar**
- ½ **teaspoon vanilla extract**
- 2 **large egg whites**

1 Preheat oven to 350°F. Grease 2 cookie sheets. Combine hazelnuts, flour, cocoa, cloves, and salt in a small bowl. Beat butter and sugar in a large mixing bowl at medium speed until light and fluffy. Beat in vanilla. Add egg whites, 1 at a time, beating well after each addition. With mixer at low speed, gradually add nut mixture, then beat at medium speed 1 minute.

2 Spoon batter into a pastry bag fitted with a ½-inch plain tip. Pipe ¾-inch rounds 2 inches apart on prepared cookie sheets. Bake 5 to 8 minutes. Transfer to wire racks to cool. Repeat process with remaining batter. Makes 9 dozen.

PER COOKIE		DAILY GOAL
Calories	25	2,000 (F), 2,500 (M)
Total Fat	2 g	60 g or less (F), 70 g or less (M)
Saturated fat	1 g	20 g or less (F), 23 g or less (M)
Cholesterol	2 mg	300 mg or less
Sodium	12 mg	2,400 mg or less
Carbohydrates	2 g	250 g or more
Protein	0 g	55 g to 90 g

COCONUT SHORTBREAD

Keep a brick of this buttery dough in your freezer so you can slice and bake them at a moment's notice.

Prep time: 7 minutes plus chilling
Baking time: 27 to 30 minutes per batch
Degree of difficulty: easy

- 1 **cup butter, softened (no substitutions)**
- ¾ **cup sugar**
- 1 **teaspoon vanilla extract**
- 1¾ **cups all-purpose flour**
- 1 **cup flaked coconut**

1 Beat butter in a large mixing bowl until creamy. Gradually beat in sugar until light and fluffy. Beat in vanilla. With mixer at low speed, gradually add flour. Stir in coconut until well combined. Shape dough into a 12x3x1-inch brick, wrap in wax paper and freeze 2 hours or refrigerate overnight.

2 Preheat oven to 300°F. Unwrap dough and slice ¼-inch thick. Arrange dough 1 inch apart on ungreased cookie sheets. Bake 27 to 30 minutes or until edges begin to turn golden. Transfer to wire racks to cool. (Can be made ahead. Wrap well and freeze up to 2 weeks.) Makes about 3½ dozen.

PER COOKIE		DAILY GOAL
Calories	85	2,000 (F), 2,500 (M)
Total Fat	5 g	60 g or less (F), 70 g or less (M)
Saturated fat	3 g	20 g or less (F), 23 g or less (M)
Cholesterol	12 mg	300 mg or less
Sodium	52 mg	2,400 mg or less
Carbohydrates	9 g	250 g or more
Protein	1 g	55 g to 90 g

31

RASPBERRY-HAZELNUT BROWNIES

Each one of these sophisticated brownies boasts of a layer of hazelnut shortbread, sweet raspberry jam, bittersweet fudge filling, and shiny chocolate glaze.

Prep time: 1 hour plus cooling
Baking time: 40 to 50 minutes
Degree of difficulty: moderate

2 **cups butter *or* margarine, divided**
¾ **cup confectioners' sugar**
2¾ **cups all-purpose flour, divided**
1 **cup hazelnuts, toasted and chopped fine (see tip, page 122)**
1 **jar (12 ounces) seedless raspberry preserves**
5 **squares (5 ounces) unsweetened chocolate, coarsely chopped**
3 **large eggs, lightly beaten**
2 **cups granulated sugar**
¼ **teaspoon salt**
1 **teaspoon vanilla extract**

6 **squares (6 ounces) semisweet chocolate, melted and cooled**
    Fresh whole raspberries, for garnish

1 Preheat oven to 350°F. For crust, line a 15½x10½-inch jelly-roll pan with foil. Beat 1 cup of the butter and the confectioners' sugar in a large mixing bowl until light and fluffy. Add 1¾ cups of the flour and the hazelnuts, beating just until mixed. Spread dough evenly in prepared pan. Bake 20 to 25 minutes or until top is lightly browned. Cool 30 minutes.

2 For filling, spread crust evenly with raspberry preserves. Refrigerate until preserves are firm, about 20 minutes.

3 Meanwhile, melt remaining 1 cup butter with unsweetened chocolate over low heat in small saucepan. Beat eggs, granulated sugar, and salt in a large mixing bowl until fluffy and thick. Beat in chocolate mixture and vanilla. Stir in remaining 1 cup flour. Pour chocolate filling over preserves. Bake 20 to 25 minutes or until toothpick inserted in filling comes out barely clean. Cool in pan on wire rack. (Can be made ahead. Wrap well and freeze up to 1 month.)

4 Lift brownies out of pan by foil edges and peel off foil from sides. Spread top evenly with melted semisweet chocolate. Garnish with fresh raspberries. Let stand until chocolate is set. Cut into 2x1-inch bars. Makes 6 dozen.

PER BROWNIE		DAILY GOAL
Calories	135	2,000 (F), 2,500 (M)
Total Fat	8 g	60 g or less (F), 70 g or less (M)
Saturated fat	4 g	20 g or less (F), 23 g or less (M)
Cholesterol	23 mg	300 mg or less
Sodium	65 mg	2,400 mg or less
Carbohydrates	16 g	250 g or more
Protein	1 g	55 g to 90 g

NOTES

_____
_____
_____
_____
_____
_____
_____
_____
_____

ALMOND TUILES

Fresh from the oven, these classic cookies from France are draped over a rolling pin to cool to give them their distinctive curved shape.

Prep time: 1½ hours
Baking time: 4 to 6 minutes per batch
● *Degree of difficulty: moderate*

- ½ **cup butter, melted and cooled, divided (no substitutions)**
- 3 **large egg whites, at room temperature**
- ½ **cup granulated sugar**
- ⅓ **cup all-purpose flour**
- 1 **teaspoon vanilla extract**
- 1 **cup blanched sliced almonds, toasted**

1 Adjust rack to lower third of oven. Preheat oven to 325°F. Grease 2 cookie sheets with some of the melted butter. Whisk whites and sugar in a mixing bowl until foamy. Whisk in flour, 5 tablespoons of the butter, and the vanilla to blend.

2 Drop batter by scant teaspoonfuls (no more than 4 or 5 per pan) 2 inches apart on a prepared cookie sheet. With a small metal spatula, spread batter into 2-inch circles. Sprinkle top with nuts.

3 Bake one sheet at a time 4 to 6 minutes or until edges are golden. Cool on pans 20 seconds. With a wide spatula, carefully remove from cookie sheet and quickly drape over a rolling pin. Repeat process with remaining batter, greasing cookie sheets as necessary. Makes 5½ dozen.

PER COOKIE		DAILY GOAL
Calories	30	2,000 (F), 2,500 (M)
Total Fat	2 g	60 g or less (F), 70 g or less (M)
Saturated fat	1 g	20 g or less (F), 23 g or less (M)
Cholesterol	4 mg	300 mg or less
Sodium	17 mg	2,400 mg or less
Carbohydrates	2 g	250 g or more
Protein	1 g	55 g to 90 g

NOTES

SWEDISH CAKES

Here's an elegant version of the old-fashioned thumbprint cookie. Fill the thumbprint with your favorite jam.

Prep time: 25 minutes
Baking time: 35 minutes per batch
O *Degree of difficulty: easy*

1 **cup butter, softened**
    (no substitutions)
½ **cup granulated sugar**
2 **large eggs, separated**
2 **cups all-purpose flour**
½ **teaspoon salt**
2 **cups finely chopped walnuts**
⅔ **cup tart cherry *or* apricot jam**

1 Preheat oven to 300°F. Grease 3 cookie sheets. Beat butter and sugar in a large mixing bowl on medium speed until light and fluffy. Beat in egg yolks, one at a time. With mixer at low speed, beat in the flour and salt.

2 Beat egg whites in a small bowl with a fork. Place nuts on a plate. Shape dough into ¾-inch balls. Dip each ball into egg whites, shaking off excess, then roll in nuts. Place 1½ inches apart on prepared cookie sheets. Indent centers of each ball with fingertip.

3 Bake 15 minutes. Remove sheets from oven. Press centers again with the handle of a wooden spoon. Fill each center with ½ teaspoon jam. Bake 20 minutes more or until golden. Transfer to wire racks to cool. Makes 5 dozen.

PER COOKIE		DAILY GOAL
Calories	90	2,000 (F), 2,500 (M)
Total Fat	6 g	60 g or less (F), 70 g or less (M)
Saturated fat	2 g	20 g or less (F), 23 g or less (M)
Cholesterol	16 mg	300 mg or less
Sodium	54 mg	2,400 mg or less
Carbohydrates	8 g	250 g or more
Protein	1 g	55 g to 90 g

BETTER WITH BUTTER

• Use only stick butter or margarine in these recipes, and take note if a recipe calls only for butter with no substitutions. Don't use reduced fat, tub products or spreads. The fat and moisture content will yield poor results.

• When a recipe calls for softening butter, don't melt it—melting will change the consistency of your dough. Simply let it sit on the counter until it reaches room temperature or microwave it on medium (50% power) for 15 seconds.

• Remember, one stick of butter equals ½ cup.

• Use other ingredients at room temperature unless otherwise noted.

CORNMEAL BISCOTTI

We've added yellow cornmeal for a tasty variation on these classic Italian cookies. Crisp and hearty, they're perfect for dunking into coffee or, as Italians prefer, a sweet wine.

Prep time: 15 minutes plus cooling
Baking time: 40 to 42 minutes
○ *Degree of difficulty: easy*

1⅓ **cups all-purpose flour**
½ **cup granulated sugar**
⅓ **cup yellow cornmeal**
¾ **teaspoon baking powder**
¼ **teaspoon baking soda**
   Pinch salt
3 **large egg whites**
¼ **cup olive oil**
½ **teaspoon grated lemon peel**
½ **teaspoon vanilla extract**
⅓ **cup whole almonds, chopped**
⅓ **cup dried tart cherries*, dried cranberries *or* raisins**

1 Preheat oven to 350°F. Combine flour, sugar, cornmeal, baking powder, baking soda, and salt in a large bowl. Stir in egg whites, oil, lemon peel, and vanilla just until combined. Stir in almonds and cherries.

2 Transfer dough to a floured surface and divide in half. Roll each half into a 10-inch log about 2 inches in diameter. Place on 2 ungreased cookie sheets and bake 30 minutes or until firm.

3 Transfer logs to a wire rack and cool 10 minutes. Slice each log diagonally into ½-inch-thick slices. Arrange slices, cut side down, on cookie sheets. Bake 5 to 6 minutes per side, or until golden and crisp. Cool completely on wire rack. Makes 2½ dozen.

*Dried tart cherries are available in some supermarkets and from American Spoon Foods. To order, call 800-222-5886.

PER COOKIE		DAILY GOAL
Calories	70	2,000 (F), 2,500 (M)
Total Fat	3 g	60 g or less (F), 70 g or less (M)
Saturated fat	0 g	20 g or less (F), 23 g or less (M)
Cholesterol	0 mg	300 mg or less
Sodium	28 mg	2,400 mg or less
Carbohydrates	10 g	250 g or more
Protein	1 g	55 g to 90 g

NOTES

PALMIERS

These ultra-flaky pastries from France are traditionally made with puff pastry dough. We've simplified the technique, but kept these buttery cookies as fancy as can be.

Prep time: 25 minutes plus chilling
Baking time: 15 to 17 minutes per batch
● *Degree of difficulty: moderate*

1½ **cups all-purpose flour**
1 **cup butter (no substitutions)**
½ **cup sour cream**
9 **tablespoons granulated sugar, divided**

1 Place flour in a bowl. Cut in butter with pastry blender until mixture resembles coarse crumbs. Stir in sour cream until pastry holds together. Divide dough in half and shape each half into a rectangle. Wrap and chill overnight.

2 Preheat oven to 375°F. Unwrap half the pastry (keep the rest refrigerated). Sprinkle 3 tablespoons of the sugar on work surface and coat pastry on all sides. Roll pastry out on the sugar into a 12x8-inch rectangle. Fold long sides in toward center to form 1-inch borders. Fold in again so edges almost meet in center. Fold together lengthwise from center to form a 12-inch log. Wrap and freeze 20 minutes. Repeat process with remaining dough and 3 tablespoons of the sugar.

3 Line 2 cookie sheets with foil. Place remaining 3 tablespoons sugar on a plate. Cut each pastry log into ¼-inch slices. Dip both sides in sugar and place slices 2 inches apart on foil. Bake 10 to 12 minutes or until edges begin to turn golden. Turn cookies over and bake 5 minutes more until golden and crisp. Transfer to wire racks to cool. Makes 8 dozen.

PER COOKIE		DAILY GOAL
Calories	30	2,000 (F), 2,500 (M)
Total Fat	2 g	60 g or less (F), 70 g or less (M)
Saturated fat	1 g	20 g or less (F), 23 g or less (M)
Cholesterol	6 mg	300 mg or less
Sodium	20 mg	2,400 mg or less
Carbohydrates	3 g	250 g or more
Protein	0 g	55 g to 90 g

NOTES

BAKING PERFECT COOKIES

• To grease cookie sheets easily, use vegetable cooking spray.

• For best results, bake one sheet of cookies at a time on the center rack of your oven. If you bake 2 sheets at once, switch the pans from one rack to the other halfway through baking.

• Remove cookies from pan and cool on wire racks.

• To help quickly remove bar cookies, line baking pans with foil.

FLORENTINES

These chewy, candy-like, saucepan cookies are a snap to make and a favorite for the holidays.

Prep time: 30 minutes plus standing
Baking time: 8 to 10 minutes per batch
○ *Degree of difficulty: easy*

⅓ **cup butter, cut up (no substitutions)**
⅔ **cup granulated sugar**
½ **cup heavy *or* whipping cream**
2 **tablespoons honey**
1⅔ **cups blanched almonds, minced**
¼ **cup candied orange peel, chopped**
¼ **cup candied cherries, chopped**
⅓ **cup all-purpose flour**
Melted semisweet chocolate, optional

1 Preheat oven to 325°F. Combine butter, sugar, cream, and honey in a medium saucepan. Cook, stirring occasionally, over low heat until butter is melted. Increase heat to medium-high and bring to a boil. Remove from heat and stir in nuts, candied fruits and flour. Cool in pan 15 minutes.

2 Grease and flour 2 cookie sheets. Drop batter by ½ teaspoonfuls 2 inches apart on cookie sheets. With a small metal spatula, spread batter into 1-inch circles.

3 Bake 8 to 10 minutes or until edges are golden. Cool on cookie sheets 30 seconds then transfer to wire racks to cool completely. Repeat process with remaining batter. Drizzle cooled cookies with melted chocolate if desired. Makes 15 dozen.

PER COOKIE		DAILY GOAL
Calories	20	2,000 (F), 2,500 (M)
Total Fat	1 g	60 g or less (F), 70 g or less (M)
Saturated fat	1 g	20 g or less (F), 23 g or less (M)
Cholesterol	2 mg	300 mg or less
Sodium	5 mg	2,400 mg or less
Carbohydrates	2 g	250 g or more
Protein	0 g	55 g to 90 g

CHERRY ALMOND PINWHEELS

These fancy cookies are easier to assemble than you might think. Chilling the dough slightly makes it a cinch to roll.

Prep time: 25 minutes plus chilling
Baking time: 12 to 13 minutes per batch
○ *Degree of difficulty: easy*

2 cups all-purpose flour
½ teaspoon baking powder
½ teaspoon salt
¾ cup butter *or* margarine, softened
¾ cup granulated sugar
1 large egg
1 teaspoon vanilla extract
¼ teaspoon almond extract
½ cup cherry preserves

1 Combine flour, baking powder, and salt in a medium bowl. Beat butter and sugar in a large mixing bowl at medium speed until light and fluffy. Beat in egg, vanilla, and almond extract. With mixer at low speed, beat in dry ingredients just until combined. Between 2 sheets of wax paper, roll dough into a 12x9-inch rectangle. Place on cookie sheet and refrigerate just until firm, 10 to 15 minutes.

2 Remove top sheet of wax paper and spread preserves evenly over dough, leaving a ½-inch border. Starting from a short side, with wax paper as a guide, roll dough up jelly-roll fashion. Wrap in wax paper and freeze at least 2 hours or refrigerate overnight.

3 Preheat oven to 375°F. Grease 2 cookie sheets. Unwrap log; with a thin, sharp knife, slice dough ¼ inch thick. Bake 12 to 13 minutes, or until edges are golden. Cool on cookie sheets 1 minute, then transfer to wire racks to cool completely. Makes 2½ dozen.

PER COOKIE		DAILY GOAL
Calories	110	2,000 (F), 2,500 (M)
Total Fat	5 g	60 g or less (F), 70 g or less (M)
Saturated fat	3 g	20 g or less (F), 23 g or less (M)
Cholesterol	19 mg	300 mg or less
Sodium	96 mg	2,400 mg or less
Carbohydrates	15 g	250 g or more
Protein	1 g	55 g to 90 g

NOTES

KEEPING THE BEAT

We recommend beating butter and sugar at medium-high speed, dry ingredients at low speed. When adding the dry ingredients, be sure not to overbeat. The dough should just be blended.

PERFECT PIES,

TARTS, AND

COBBLERS

Whether on the bottom or the top, fruit-, nut-, or cream-filled, with this peck of perfect pies, tarts, and cobblers, it's all in the crust. Who can resist the down-home comfort of our Old-Fashioned Apple, deep dish True Blueberry, or lattice-topped Classic Tart Cherry pies straight from the farm? Our sophisticated tarts are open-faced and easy to prepare. You'll love the choices: Pear and Apple Tart Tatin with a crown of caramel, Satin Berry Tart cream-filled, with summery flavors, or individual Espresso Pecan Tarts that are perfect for the holidays.

OLD-FASHIONED APPLE PIE

Everyone's favorite—a double crust apple pie fresh from the oven, bubbling with sweet heavy cream.

Prep time: 35 minutes plus chilling
Baking time: 70 to 75 minutes
Degree of difficulty: moderate

Flaky Vinegar Pastry for a 9-inch, double-crust pie (recipe at right)
- ½ **cup granulated sugar**
- 3 **tablespoons flour**
- 1 **teaspoon cinnamon**
- ⅛ **teaspoon nutmeg**
- ⅛ **teaspoon salt**
- 2½ **pounds tart apples (Golden Delicious, Jonathan, *or* Pippin), peeled, cut into ½-inch wedges**
- 2 **teaspoons fresh lemon juice**
- 2 **tablespoons butter *or* margarine, cut up**
- ½ **cup heavy *or* whipping cream**

1 Preheat oven to 425°F. Combine sugar, flour, cinnamon, nutmeg, and salt in a large bowl. Add apples and lemon juice, tossing well to blend. Set aside.

2 On a lightly floured surface, roll larger pastry disk into a 12-inch circle and fit into a 9-inch pie pan, leaving a 1-inch overhang. Spoon apple mixture into pie pan. Dot with butter.

3 Roll remaining pastry into an 12-inch circle. Cut into ten 1-inch-wide strips and arrange in a lattice pattern on top of apples. Trim lattice ends and flute edge of pastry.

4 Place pie on cookie sheet and bake 15 minutes. Reduce oven temperature to 375°F. Bake 45 to 50 minutes more or until apples are tender. Pour cream evenly over exposed filling. Bake 10 minutes more or until filling is bubbly and crust is golden. Cool completely on wire rack or serve warm. Makes 8 servings.

PER SERVING		DAILY GOAL
Calories	480	2,000 (F), 2,500 (M)
Total Fat	25 g	60 g or less (F), 70 g or less (M)
Saturated fat	14 g	20 g or less (F), 23 g or less (M)
Cholesterol	59 mg	300 mg or less
Sodium	324 mg	2,400 mg or less
Carbohydrates	61 g	250 g or more
Protein	4 g	55 g to 90 g

FLAKY VINEGAR PASTRY

This super flaky pie crust contains Grandma's secret ingredient: vinegar! (An equal amount of fresh lemon juice will do the same trick.)

- 2 **cups all-purpose flour**
- ½ **teaspoon salt**
- ½ **cup chilled butter *or* margarine, cut up**
- 3 **tablespoons vegetable shortening**
- 1 **tablespoon distilled white vinegar**
- 4 **to 5 tablespoons ice water**

1 Combine flour and salt in a large bowl. Gradually add butter and shortening, tossing gently until all pieces are coated with flour. With pastry blender or 2 knives, cut in butter until mixture resembles coarse crumbs. Sprinkle with vinegar, then add ice water, 1 tablespoon at a time, tossing vigorously with a fork until pastry just begins to hold together.

2 On a smooth surface, shape pastry into a ball, kneading lightly if necessary. Divide pastry into 2 balls, one slightly larger than the other. For 2 single crusts, divide dough into equal-size portions. Flatten into 2 thick disks. Wrap tightly in plastic wrap and refrigerate 1 hour or overnight. Makes 1 double crust or 2 single crusts.

TRUE BLUEBERRY PIE

Bubbly and gorgeous, this pie is summer's best. The filling can be prepared with either fresh or unthawed frozen blueberries.

Prep time: 25 minutes plus chilling
Baking time: 70 minutes
● *Degree of difficulty: moderate*

Classic Pastry for a 9-inch, double-crust pie (recipe at right)
5   **cups blueberries**
⅔   **cup plus 1 teaspoon granulated sugar**
¼   **cup all-purpose flour**
1   **teaspoon grated lemon peel**
¼   **teaspoon cinnamon**
      Pinch cloves
2   **tablespoons fresh lemon juice**
1   **tablespoon butter *or* margarine**
2   **teaspoons milk**

1   Place a cookie sheet on the middle rack of oven. Preheat oven to 450°F. Combine blueberries, ⅔ cup of the sugar, flour, lemon peel, cinnamon, and cloves in a large bowl, tossing well to blend. Set aside.

2   On a lightly floured surface, roll larger pastry disk into a 12-inch circle and fit into a 9-inch pie pan. Spoon blueberry mixture into pie pan. Dot with butter.

3   Roll remaining pastry into a 10-inch circle and place on top of filling. With a small sharp knife, cut vents in top pastry for steam. Trim edge and flute. Brush pastry with milk and sprinkle with remaining 1 teaspoon sugar.

4   Place pie on cookie sheet and bake 20 minutes. Reduce oven temperature to 375°F. Bake 50 minutes more or until filling is bubbly in center. (Cover pie loosely with foil, if necessary, to prevent overbrowning.) Cool on wire rack at least 1 hour before serving. Makes 8 servings.

PER SERVING		DAILY GOAL
Calories	405	2,000 (F), 2,500 (M)
Total Fat	18 g	60 g or less (F), 70 g or less (M)
Saturated fat	8 g	20 g or less (F), 23 g or less (M)
Cholesterol	24 mg	300 mg or less
Sodium	236 mg	2,400 mg or less
Carbohydrates	58 g	250 g or more
Protein	4 g	55 g to 90 g

CLASSIC PASTRY

2   **cups all-purpose flour**
½   **teaspoon salt**
⅓   **cup cold butter *or* margarine, cut up**
⅓   **cup vegetable shortening, chilled**
5   **to 6 tablespoons ice water**

1   Combine flour and salt in a medium bowl. Gradually add butter and shortening, tossing gently until all pieces are coated with flour. With pastry blender or 2 knives, cut in butter until mixture resembles coarse crumbs. Add ice water, 1 tablespoon at a time, tossing vigorously with a fork until pastry just begins to hold together.

2   On a smooth surface, shape pastry into a ball, kneading lightly if necessary. Divide pastry into 2 balls, one slightly larger than the other. For 2 single crusts, divide dough into equal-size portions. Flatten into 2 thick disks. Wrap tightly in plastic wrap and refrigerate 1 hour or overnight. Makes 1 double crust or 2 single crusts.

CLASSIC TART CHERRY PIE

This is truly the king of fruit pies, especially when the filling features fabulous, fresh tart cherries! Tart cherries are available from late June through July and they're quite perishable, so refrigerate them and use within a day or two. Be sure to wash the fruit just before using and discard any shriveled or mushy fruit. *Also pictured on page 42.*

Prep time: 25 minutes plus chilling
Baking time: 60 to 70 minutes
Degree of difficulty: moderate

Flaky Vinegar or Classic Pastry for a 9-inch, double-crust pie (recipes pages 44-45)
1 **cup plus 1 tablespoon granulated sugar**
3 **tablespoons cornstarch**
⅛ **teaspoon cinnamon**
 Pinch salt
5 **cups fresh pitted sour cherries, 1½ pounds frozen cherries *or* 2 cans (16 ounces each) pitted sour cherries***

2 **tablespoons fresh lemon juice**
1 **tablespoon butter *or* margarine, cut up**

1 Preheat oven to 425°F. Between 2 sheets of wax paper, roll larger piece of pastry into an 11-inch circle and fit into a 9-inch pie pan, leaving a 1-inch overhang.

2 Combine 1 cup of the sugar, cornstarch, cinnamon, and salt in a large bowl. Add cherries and lemon juice; toss gently to blend. Spoon into pie pan. Dot with butter.

3 Between 2 sheets of wax paper, roll remaining pastry into a 9-inch circle. Cut into ½-inch-wide strips and arrange in a lattice pattern on top of cherries. Trim lattice ends and flute edge of pastry. Sprinkle lattice with remaining 1 tablespoon sugar.

4 Place pie on cookie sheet and bake 20 minutes. Reduce oven temperature to 375°F. Bake 40 to 50 minutes more or until filling is bubbly in center. (Cover pie loosely with foil, if necessary, to prevent overbrowning.) Cool on wire rack at least 1 hour before serving. Makes 8 servings.

*For canned cherries: Drain cherries, reserving ½ cup juice. Combine 1 cup sugar, 3 tablespoons cornstarch, ⅛ teaspoon cinnamon, and a pinch of salt in a medium saucepan. Stir in reserved cherry juice and 2 tablespoons fresh lemon juice. Bring to boil over medium heat, stirring constantly; boil 1 minute. Remove from heat; stir in cherries. Cool completely. Proceed with recipe.

PER SERVING		DAILY GOAL
Calories	425	2,000 (F), 2,500 (M)
Total Fat	19 g	60 g or less (F), 70 g or less (M)
Saturated fat	5 g	20 g or less (F), 23 g or less (M)
Cholesterol	4 mg	300 mg or less
Sodium	102 mg	2,400 mg or less
Carbohydrates	61 g	250 g or more
Protein	4 g	55 g to 90 g

NOTES

_____

_____

_____

_____

_____

_____

_____

_____

CRISP NECTARINE-PHYLLO PIE

We've drastically reduced the fat in this inventive summer fruit pie by using sugar-glazed phyllo dough for the crust. To keep it flaky, fill with fruit just before serving.

Prep time: 20 minutes plus standing
Baking time: 10 minutes
○ *Degree of difficulty: easy*

- 4 **sheets phyllo dough**
- 4 **teaspoons vegetable oil**
- 4 **teaspoons plus 3 tablespoons granulated sugar**
- 4 **cups (1½ pounds) thinly sliced ripe nectarines**
- 1 **tablespoon fresh lemon juice**
- 1 **tablespoon orange-flavored liqueur**
- 1 **container (8 ounces) plain, low-fat yogurt**
- 1 **tablespoon honey**
- ¼ **cup grated orange peel**

1 Preheat oven to 375°F. Place 1 phyllo sheet in a 9-inch pie plate, letting sides overhang. Brush lightly with oil and sprinkle with 1 teaspoon of the sugar. Place another phyllo sheet diagonally on top; brush lightly with oil and sprinkle with 1 teaspoon of the sugar. Repeat layering phyllo to form a pinwheel, brushing each piece lightly with oil and sprinkling with sugar. Bake 10 minutes or until golden. Cool on wire rack.

2 Meanwhile, toss nectarines with remaining 3 tablespoons sugar, lemon juice, and liqueur in a large bowl. Let stand at room temperature up to 1 hour.

3 Combine yogurt with honey and orange peel in a small bowl. Spoon fruit into pastry shell and serve with yogurt. Makes 6 servings.

PER SERVING		DAILY GOAL
Calories	200	2,000 (F), 2,500 (M)
Total Fat	4 g	60 g or less (F), 70 g or less (M)
Saturated fat	1 g	20 g or less (F), 23 g or less (M)
Cholesterol	2 mg	300 mg or less
Sodium	83 mg	2,400 mg or less
Carbohydrates	38 g	250 g or more
Protein	4 g	55 g to 90 g

NOTES

AUTUMN PLUM PIE

You won't need to peel the plums for this luscious pie. It's the balance of sweet fruit and tart skin that makes the filling so scrumptious.

Prep time: 1 hour
Baking time: 1¼ hours
Degree of difficulty: moderate

1   **cup granulated sugar**
⅓   **cup all-purpose flour**
¼   **teaspoon ginger**
¼   **teaspoon cinnamon**
6   **cups (2¼ pounds) thinly sliced plums**
    Flaky Vinegar or Classic Pastry for a 9-inch, double-crust pie (recipes pages 44-45)

1 Preheat oven to 425°F. Combine sugar, flour, ginger, and cinnamon in a large bowl. Add plums and toss until well combined.

2 Between 2 sheets of wax paper, roll larger piece of pastry into an 11-inch circle and fit into a 9-inch pie pan, leaving a 1-inch overhang. Spoon plum filling into pie pan.

3 Between 2 sheets of wax paper, roll remaining pastry into a 9½-inch circle. Cut into ½-inch-wide strips and arrange in a lattice pattern on top of plums. Trim lattice ends and flute edge of pastry.

4 Place pie on a cookie sheet and bake 15 minutes. Reduce oven temperature to 375°F. Bake 1 hour more or until filling is bubbly near the center. (Cover pie loosely with foil, if necessary, to prevent over-browning.) Cool on wire rack at least 1 hour before serving. Makes 8 servings.

PER SERVING		DAILY GOAL
Calories	410	2,000 (F), 2,500 (M)
Total Fat	16 g	60 g or less (F), 70 g or less (M)
Saturated fat	4 g	20 g or less (F), 23 g or less (M)
Cholesterol	20 mg	300 mg or less
Sodium	234 mg	2,400 mg or less
Carbohydrates	65 g	250 g or more
Protein	4 g	55 g to 90 g

THE BIG CHILL: FROSTY FRUIT PIES

• Freezing unbaked fruit pies preserves their fresh flavor. Prepare the fruit filling as usual, adding an extra tablespoon of all-purpose flour per pie. Finish the pie as directed, however, for a double crust pie, do not cut vents in the top crust. Wrap well in freezer wrap and freeze up to three months.

• To bake a frozen pie, preheat oven. Unwrap pie, place on a cookie sheet and cut vents. Bake unthawed, adding 15 to 20 minutes to the baking time in the recipe.

• To freeze a baked fruit pie, cool completely and wrap well in freezer wrap. Freeze up to three months. Thaw at room temperature 30 minutes. Unwrap and bake in a preheated 350°F. oven 30 minutes.

BANANA-ALMOND CREAM PIE

This sublime custard pie comes from Sarabeth Levine, a fabulous baker and restaurant owner in New York City.

Prep time: 1 hour plus chilling
Baking time: 25 minutes
Degree of difficulty: moderate

¾ **cup unsalted butter, softened (no substitutions)**
½ **cup granulated sugar**
1 **large egg**
1¼ **cups (6 ounces) ground toasted almonds**
1½ **cups all-purpose flour**
¼ **teaspoon salt, divided**
⅛ **teaspoon baking powder**
1½ **teaspoons unflavored gelatin**
3 **tablespoons cold water**
½ **vanilla bean *or* 1 tablespoon vanilla extract**
1 **cup milk**
⅓ **cup granulated sugar**
1 **tablespoon cornstarch**
3 **large egg yolks**

1¼ **cups heavy *or* whipping cream, divided**
4 **ripe bananas, sliced**
⅓ **cup confectioners' sugar**
1 **ripe banana, sliced, for garnish**

1 For almond pastry, beat butter and the ½ cup granulated sugar in a large mixing bowl until light and fluffy. Beat in egg until smooth. Combine almonds, flour, ⅛ teaspoon of the salt, and baking powder in a medium bowl; stir into butter mixture until well combined. Form pastry into 2 thick disks. (Freeze 1 disk for later use.) Refrigerate remaining pastry 1 hour. Between 2 sheets wax paper, roll pastry into an 11-inch circle and fit into a 9-inch pie pan; trim and flute edge. Freeze 20 minutes.

2 Meanwhile, preheat oven to 350°F. Line frozen pastry shell with foil and fill with dried beans or uncooked rice. Bake 15 minutes. Remove foil and beans or rice. Bake pastry 10 minutes more or until golden. Cool completely on wire rack.

3 For filling, sprinkle gelatin over water in a small bowl; let soften 5 minutes. Split vanilla bean in half lengthwise, scrape out seeds. Place seeds and pod in medium saucepan with milk; bring to a boil. Meanwhile, combine the ⅓ cup granulated

sugar, cornstarch, and remaining ⅛ teaspoon salt in a small bowl. Whisk in egg yolks until smooth. Gradually whisk hot milk into yolk mixture. Return to saucepan and bring to a boil, whisking constantly. Reduce heat to low, cook 2 minutes more, whisking. Remove from heat and stir in softened gelatin until completely dissolved. (Stir in vanilla extract, if using.) Refrigerate, stirring occasionally, until mixture mounds when dropped from a spoon, 30 to 45 minutes. Remove vanilla bean pod.

4 Beat ¾ cup of the cream in a mixing bowl to soft peaks. Gently fold into gelatin mixture with a rubber spatula. Fold in bananas and pour into cooled crust. Refrigerate until set, 2 hours.

5 To serve, beat remaining ½ cup cream in a mixing bowl to soft peaks; add confectioners' sugar and continue beating until stiff. Pipe or spoon decoratively on top of pie. Garnish with additional sliced banana. Makes 10 servings.

PER SERVING		DAILY GOAL	
Calories	575	2,000 (F), 2,500 (M)	
Total Fat	37 g	60 g or less (F), 70 g or less (M)	
Saturated fat	17 g	20 g or less (F), 23 g or less (M)	
Cholesterol	166 mg	300 mg or less	
Sodium	98 mg	2,400 mg or less	
Carbohydrates	55 g	250 g or more	
Protein	9 g	55 g to 90 g	

SLICE OF LEMON PIE

For citrus lovers only, this custard pie of Shaker origin boasts an unusual filling of sliced lemons.

Prep time: 45 minutes plus chilling
Baking time: 35 to 40 minutes
Degree of difficulty: moderate

- 6 **sugar cubes**
- 2 **small lemons, rinsed**
  Flaky Vinegar or Classic Pastry
  for a 9-inch, double-crust pie
  (recipes pages 44-45)
- 2 **cups granulated sugar**
- ⅓ **cup all-purpose flour**
- ¼ **teaspoon salt**
- ⅔ **cup water**
- 2 **tablespoons butter *or* margarine,**
  softened
- 3 **large eggs**
- 1 **teaspoon grated orange peel**

1 Preheat oven to 400°F. Rub sugar cubes over lemons to extract oil from peel. Place cubes in a plastic bag and crush with a rolling pin; set aside. With a sharp knife, cut peel and white pith from lemons; discard. Slice lemons ⅛ inch thick and remove seeds.

2 On a lightly floured surface, roll larger piece of pastry into a 13-inch circle and fit into a 9-inch pie pan, letting pastry overhang edge. Roll remaining pastry into a 10-inch circle and cut vents in top pastry for steam. Set aside.

3 Combine granulated sugar, flour, and salt in a large bowl. Whisk in water, butter, eggs, and orange peel. Stir in the lemon slices. Pour into pie pan. Top with remaining pastry; flute edge. If desired, cut out lemon shapes from pastry scraps to decorate top. Sprinkle with crushed sugar cubes. Bake 35 to 40 minutes until filling is bubbly and crust is golden. Cool on a wire rack at least 2 hours before serving. Makes 8 servings.

PER SERVING		DAILY GOAL
Calories	500	2,000 (F), 2,500 (M)
Total Fat	20 g	60 g or less (F), 70 g or less (M)
Saturated fat	6 g	20 g or less (F), 23 g or less (M)
Cholesterol	87 mg	300 mg or less
Sodium	397 mg	2,400 mg or less
Carbohydrates	78 g	250 g or more
Protein	6 g	55 g to 90 g

BLIND BAKING

What's the secret to a perfect pastry shell? Here's how to keep the crust from slipping or shrinking:

1. Prick the bottom of the pastry shell with a fork and freeze until firm, 20 minutes. Line pastry with foil and weight it down with pie weights, dried beans, or uncooked rice, and bake until edges of pie shell are set. (Keep the beans and rice, they can be used again and again.)

2. Remove the foil and beans or uncooked rice and continue to bake until the crust is golden. If the pastry puffs up during baking, prick it again with a fork.

3. After removing your pie shell or a baked pie from the oven, cool completely on a wire rack before filling. This air circulation keeps the bottom crust crisp.

4. The pie crust can be covered and frozen up to one week before filling. Let it thaw completely at room temperature, then crisp it in a 350° oven for 10 minutes.

PEAR AND APPLE TART TATIN

The combination of pear and apple adds a new dimension of flavor to this classic upside down French fruit tart.

Prep time: 30 minutes plus chilling
Baking time: 35 minutes
● *Degree of difficulty: moderate*

1 **cup all-purpose flour**
2 **teaspoons granulated sugar**
   Pinch salt
⅓ **cup cold butter, cut up**
   (no substitutions)
3 **to 4 tablespoons ice water**
6 **tablespoons butter, softened,**
   divided (no substitutions)
8 **tablespoons granulated sugar,**
   divided
3 **ripe Anjou *or* Bartlett pears,**
   peeled, cored, and quartered
3 **tart green *or* Golden Delicious**
   apples, peeled, cored, and
   quartered

1 For pastry, mix flour, the 2 teaspoons sugar, and salt in a medium bowl. Cut in cold butter with pastry blender or 2 knives until mixture resembles coarse crumbs. Add water 1 tablespoon at a time, tossing with a fork until pastry comes together. Shape into a thick disk. Wrap in plastic wrap and refrigerate 1 hour or overnight.

2 For filling, on a lightly floured surface, roll pastry ⅜ inch thick and cut a 9-inch circle. Freeze 1 hour on a cookie sheet lined with wax paper.

3 Preheat oven to 375°F. Spread 4 tablespoons of the softened butter over bottom and sides of a 10-inch cast iron skillet. Sprinkle bottom and sides with 5 tablespoons of the sugar. Alternate apple and pear quarters, cored side up and wide end pointing out, in tight concentric circles in skillet. Arrange remaining apple and pear quarters in center. Dot with remaining 2 tablespoons of softened butter and sprinkle with remaining 3 tablespoons sugar. Cook over medium-high heat, shaking and swirling skillet frequently, until sugar is caramelized and golden brown, about 15 minutes.

4 Place a cookie sheet on center oven rack. Invert frozen crust over fruit in skillet and remove wax paper. Place skillet on cookie sheet and bake about 35 minutes or until crust is well browned.

5 Remove skillet from oven. Immediately invert tart onto serving dish. Serve warm or at room temperature. Makes 8 servings.

PER SERVING		DAILY GOAL	
Calories	315	2,000 (F), 2,500 (M)	
Total Fat	17 g	60 g or less (F), 70 g or less (M)	
Saturated fat	10 g	20 g or less (F), 23 g or less (M)	
Cholesterol	44 mg	300 mg or less	
Sodium	182 mg	2,400 mg or less	
Carbohydrates	42 g	250 g or more	
Protein	2 g	55 g to 90 g	

NOTES

_____

_____

_____

_____

_____

_____

_____

_____

CLASSIC PUMPKIN PIE

We've added an extra touch of spice in both the pastry and filling of this favorite holiday pie.

Prep time: 15 minutes plus chilling
Baking time: 45 to 50 minutes
○ *Degree of difficulty: easy*

1½	**cups all-purpose flour**
⅛	**teaspoon mace**
½	**cup cold butter *or* margarine, cut up**
2	**tablespoons shortening**
½	**teaspoon vanilla extract**
3	**to 5 tablespoons ice water**
1	**can (16 ounces) solid-pack pumpkin**
1	**cup half-and-half cream**
3	**large eggs**
⅔	**cup firmly packed brown sugar**
1	**tablespoon brandy**
1	**teaspoon cinnamon**
½	**teaspoon ginger**
½	**teaspoon salt**
¼	**teaspoon ground white pepper**
	Pinch cloves

1 For spice pastry, combine flour and mace in a medium bowl. Gradually add butter and shortening, one piece at a time, tossing gently until all pieces are coated with flour. With pastry blender or 2 knives, cut in butter until mixture resembles coarse crumbs. Combine vanilla with 3 tablespoons ice water. Sprinkle over flour, tossing vigorously with a fork and adding additional water, 1 tablespoon at a time, if necessary, until pastry just begins to hold together. On a smooth surface, shape pastry into a ball, kneading lightly if necessary; flatten into a thick disk. Wrap tightly in plastic wrap and refrigerate 1 hour or overnight.

2 Adjust oven rack to lowest position. Preheat oven to 375°F. Between 2 sheets wax paper, roll pastry into an 11-inch circle and fit into a 9-inch pie pan, letting pastry overhang edge. Trim and flute. Freeze 15 minutes.

3 For filling, stir all remaining ingredients together in a large bowl until well combined. Pour into pastry shell. Bake 45 to 50 minutes or until a small, sharp knife inserted in center comes out clean. Cool completely on a wire rack. Makes 8 servings.

PER SERVING		DAILY GOAL
Calories	375	2,000 (F), 2,500 (M)
Total Fat	20 g	60 g or less (F), 70 g or less (M)
Saturated fat	10 g	20 g or less (F), 23 g or less (M)
Cholesterol	122 mg	300 mg or less
Sodium	300 mg	2,400 mg or less
Carbohydrates	43 g	250 g or more
Protein	6 g	55 g to 90 g

CARAMEL PIE

The key to the wonderful flavor and color of this satiny custard pie is caramelizing the granulated sugar, then stirring it into the milk.

Prep time: 1 hour plus chilling
Baking time: 20 to 22 minutes
◑ *Degree of difficulty: moderate*

1½	**cups all-purpose flour**
½	**teaspoon salt, divided**
6	**tablespoons cold butter *or* margarine, cut up**
2	**tablespoons shortening**
4	**to 6 tablespoons ice water**
¾	**cup plus 2 tablespoons granulated sugar**
¼	**cup water**
¼	**cup cornstarch**

2 **cups milk**
1 **cup heavy _or_ whipping cream**
4 **large egg yolks**
2 **teaspoons vanilla extract**

Praline (optional)
¾ **cup sugar**
¼ **cup water**
½ **cup sliced almonds**
   Whipped cream (optional)

1 For pastry, combine flour and ¼ teaspoon of the salt in a medium bowl. Gradually add butter and shortening, one piece at a time, tossing gently until all pieces are coated with flour. With pastry blender or 2 knives, cut in butter until mixture resembles coarse crumbs. Add ice water, 1 tablespoon at a time, tossing vigorously with a fork until pastry just begins to hold together. On a smooth surface, shape pastry into a ball, kneading lightly if necessary; flatten into a thick disk. Wrap tightly in plastic wrap and refrigerate 1 hour or overnight.

2 Preheat oven to 425°F. On a lightly floured surface, roll pastry into a 13-inch circle and fit into a 9-inch pie pan, letting pastry overhang edge. Trim and flute. Prick bottom with a fork. Freeze 15 minutes.

3 Line frozen pastry shell with foil and fill with dried beans or uncooked rice. Bake 12 minutes. Remove foil and beans or rice. Bake pastry 8 to 10 minutes more or until deep golden. Cool completely on a wire rack.

4 For filling, combine ¾ cup of the sugar and the ¼ cup water in a large saucepan. Cook over medium heat or until sugar is melted and turns a deep amber color, about 12 to 15 minutes. Do not stir. (Be careful not to burn.)

5 Meanwhile, combine remaining 2 tablespoons sugar, cornstarch and remaining ¼ teaspoon salt in a large bowl. Gradually whisk in milk and cream until smooth. When sugar is caramelized, remove saucepan from heat. Carefully add cream mixture, whisking in a steady stream, until blended. (Mixture will boil vigorously.) Return to heat and bring to boiling; stirring gently to dissolve any remaining hardened caramel. Boil 1 minute, remove from heat.

6 Beat egg yolks lightly in a small bowl. Gradually whisk in 1 cup hot filling. Return to saucepan, whisking constantly. Boil 1 minute more. Remove from heat and stir in vanilla. Immediately pour filling into baked pastry crust. Cool 15 minutes on a wire rack. Cover surface of filling and refrigerate at least 3 hours. Just before serving, garnish with Praline and whipped cream if desired. Makes 8 servings.

Praline: Line 1 cookie sheet with foil and oil lightly. Combine sugar and water in a medium saucepan. Cook over medium heat until sugar is melted and turns a deep amber color, about 12 to 15 minutes (_do not stir_). Add almonds, swirling pan to coat nuts. Immediately pour hot mixture onto prepared pan in an even ⅛-inch-thick layer. Cool completely. Peel off foil and crack into large serving pieces.

PER SERVING
WITHOUT PRALINE
OR WHIPPED CREAM

		DAILY GOAL
Calories	385	2,000 (F), 2,500 (M)
Total Fat	23 g	60 g or less (F), 70 g or less (M)
Saturated fat	11 g	20 g or less (F), 23 g or less (M)
Cholesterol	156 mg	300 mg or less
Sodium	230 mg	2,400 mg or less
Carbohydrates	40 g	250 g or more
Protein	5 g	55 g to 90 g

55

CRANBERRY-ALMOND TART

This fresh cranberry topping forms a ruby crown over a scrumptious marzipan filling wrapped in a shortbread crust. Because the flavor is so intense, a very small slice will satisfy. It's the perfect finale to your Thanksgiving feast.

Prep time: 45 minutes plus chilling
Baking time: 40 to 42 minutes
⊖ *Degree of difficulty: moderate*

10 **tablespoons butter, softened (no substitutions)**
 6 **tablespoons confectioners' sugar**
1⅓ **cups all-purpose flour**
 ⅓ **cup butter, softened (no substitutions)**
 ¼ **cup almond paste**
 ⅓ **cup granulated sugar**
 1 **large egg**
 1 **teaspoon vanilla extract**
 ½ **teaspoon grated lemon peel**
 ¼ **teaspoon salt**
 ½ **cup granulated sugar**
 6 **tablespoons water**

 2 **cups cranberries, divided**
 4 **teaspoons cornstarch**

1 Preheat oven to 350°F. For shortbread crust, beat the 10 tablespoons butter and confectioners' sugar in a large mixing bowl until light and fluffy. With mixer at low speed, gradually add flour, beating until well combined. With lightly floured fingers, press dough into a 9½-inch tart pan with a removable bottom. Prick bottom of pastry with a fork. Bake 20 to 22 minutes or until very lightly golden. Cool completely on a wire rack.

2 For filling, beat the ⅓ cup butter and almond paste in a clean mixing bowl until light, fluffy, and completely smooth. Gradually add the ⅓ cup sugar until well combined. Beat in egg, vanilla, lemon peel, and salt. Spread evenly in prepared pastry. Bake 20 minutes or until top of filling is golden. Cool on wire rack.

3 Meanwhile, for topping, heat the remaining ½ cup sugar and 6 tablespoons water to boiling in a medium saucepan; reduce heat and simmer until sugar is dissolved. Add 1 cup of the cranberries and simmer 5 minutes. Dissolve cornstarch in 2 tablespoons water in a cup and stir into cranberry mixture. Bring to a boil, reduce heat and simmer, stirring, 2 minutes. Stir in remaining 1 cup cranberries. Cool completely. Spoon cranberry topping over tart. Refrigerate at least 4 hours. (Can be made ahead. Cover and refrigerate up to 24 hours.) Remove tart from pan before serving. Makes 16 servings.

PER SERVING		DAILY GOAL
Calories	215	2,000 (F), 2,500 (M)
Total Fat	12 g	60 g or less (F), 70 g or less (M)
Saturated fat	7 g	20 g or less (F), 23 g or less (M)
Cholesterol	43 mg	300 mg or less
Sodium	150 mg	2,400 mg or less
Carbohydrates	25 g	250 g or more
Protein	2 g	55 g to 90 g

ESPRESSO PECAN TARTS

These precious little tarts are perfect for the holiday table. We've added the sophisticated taste of espresso and coffee liqueur to bring out the rich flavor in the pecan filling.

Prep time: 45 minutes plus chilling
Baking time: 30 to 35 minutes
⊖ *Degree of difficulty: moderate*

2 cups all-purpose flour
3 tablespoons granulated sugar
¼ teaspoon salt
½ cup cold, unsalted butter, cut up
   (no substitutions)
2 large egg yolks
5 tablespoons ice water
1 teaspoon instant espresso powder
1 tablespoon boiling water
2 large eggs, lightly beaten
⅔ cup firmly packed brown sugar
⅔ cup light corn syrup
2 tablespoons butter, melted
   (no substitutions)
2 tablespoons coffee-flavored liqueur
½ teaspoon vanilla extract
2 cups pecan halves, toasted

Coffee Whipped Cream
1 cup heavy or whipping cream
2 tablespoons confectioners' sugar
2 tablespoons coffee-flavored liqueur
   Chocolate-covered coffee beans, for
   garnish

1 For pastry, combine flour, granulated sugar, and salt in a medium bowl. Gradually add cold butter, 1 piece at a time, tossing gently until all pieces are coated with flour. With pastry blender or 2 knives, cut in butter until mixture resembles coarse crumbs. Whisk egg yolks and ice water until blended in a small bowl. Add yolk mixture, tossing vigorously with a fork until pastry just begins to hold together. On a smooth surface, shape pastry into a ball, kneading lightly if necessary. Flatten into a thick disk. Wrap tightly in plastic wrap and refrigerate 1 hour or overnight.

2 Preheat oven to 425°F. Divide pastry into 6 equal pieces. On a lightly floured surface, roll each piece into a 6-inch circle. Transfer each pastry circle to a 4¾-inch individual tartlet pan with a removable bottom. Gently press pastry with fingertips along bottom and up edge of pans. With scissors, trim pastry to ½ inch above edge. Fold overhanging pastry into side of crust and gently press edge up to extend ¼ inch above side of pan. (Or roll pastry to a 14-inch circle. Fit into a 12-inch tart pan with removable bottom.) Freeze 15 minutes.

3 Line frozen pastry shells with foil and fill with dried beans or uncooked rice. Place on cookie sheets and bake for 10 minutes. Remove foil and beans or rice.

Bake tart shells 8 to 10 minutes more or until golden. Cool on a wire rack. Reduce oven temperature to 350°F.

4 For filling, dissolve espresso powder in boiling water in a medium bowl. Whisk in eggs, brown sugar, corn syrup, melted butter, liqueur, and vanilla; stir until just combined. Fold in pecans.

5 Spoon filling evenly into tart shells and arrange on cookie sheets. Bake 30 to 35 minutes or until filling is just set. Cool tarts on a wire rack 10 minutes, then remove from pans and cool completely. (Can be made ahead. Wrap and freeze up to 2 weeks. Thaw at room temperature 6 to 8 hours.) Serve tarts with a dollop of Coffee Whipped Cream and garnish with chocolate-covered coffee beans. Makes 12 servings.

Coffee Whipped Cream: Beat all ingredients in a large mixing bowl until soft peaks form.

PER TART WITH CREAM		DAILY GOAL
Calories	495	2,000 (F), 2,500 (M)
Total Fat	30 g	60 g or less (F), 70 g or less (M)
Saturated fat	12 g	20 g or less (F), 23 g or less (M)
Cholesterol	124 mg	300 mg or less
Sodium	180 mg	2,400 mg or less
Carbohydrates	52 g	250 g or more
Protein	6 g	55 g to 90 g

TRIPLE-NUT CARAMEL TART

This tart will remind you of pecan pie, but with a few surprises: The sugar is caramelized for flavor and color, and the crunch comes from three kinds of nuts.

Prep time: 50 minutes plus chilling
Baking time: 52 to 55 minutes
Degree of difficulty: moderate

- 1¼ **cups all-purpose flour**
- ¼ **teaspoon salt, divided**
- 4 **tablespoons cold butter, cut up (no substitutions)**
- 2 **tablespoons vegetable shortening**
- 3 to 4 **tablespoons ice water**
- ½ **cup granulated sugar**
  Water
- ¾ **cup light corn syrup**
- 2 **large eggs, lightly beaten**
- 2 **tablespoons butter, melted (no substitutions)**
- 1 **tablespoon dark rum**
- ⅓ **cup walnuts, coarsely chopped**
- ⅓ **cup pecans, coarsely chopped**
- ⅓ **cup sliced almonds**

1 For pastry, combine flour and ⅛ teaspoon of the salt in a medium bowl. Cut in cold butter with pastry blender or 2 knives until mixture resembles fine crumbs. Add water 1 tablespoon at a time, tossing with a fork until pastry comes together. Shape into a thick disk. Wrap in plastic wrap and refrigerate 30 minutes.

2 Preheat oven to 375°F. On a lightly floured surface, roll pastry into an 11-inch circle. Fit into a 9½-inch tart pan with a removable bottom or 9-inch pie plate. Gently press pastry with fingertips along bottom and up side of pan. With scissors, trim pastry to 1 inch above edge. Fold overhanging pastry in to side of crust and gently press edge up to extend ¼ inch above side of pan; trim edge. Freeze 10 minutes.

3 Line pastry with foil and fill with dried beans or uncooked rice. Bake 15 minutes. Remove foil and beans or rice; bake 12 to 15 minutes more or until pastry is golden brown. Cool on a wire rack.

4 For filling, combine sugar and 1 tablespoon water in a medium saucepan. Cook over medium heat just until sugar is dissolved. Continue cooking without stirring until syrup is a caramel color.

Remove from heat. With a long-handled spoon, carefully add ⅓ cup water, stirring until smooth (mixture will bubble vigorously).

5 Reduce oven temperature to 350°F. Whisk together cooled caramel, corn syrup, eggs, melted butter, rum, and remaining ⅛ teaspoon salt in a medium bowl until smooth.

6 Spread nuts in an even layer in pastry crust; place on cookie sheet. Pour in caramel filling. Bake 25 minutes or until center is just set. Cool. Remove tart from pan before serving. Makes 8 servings.

PER SERVING		DAILY GOAL
Calories	420	2,000 (F), 2,500 (M)
Total Fat	21 g	60 g or less (F), 70 g or less (M)
Saturated fat	7 g	20 g or less (F), 23 g or less (M)
Cholesterol	76 mg	300 mg or less
Sodium	211 mg	2,400 mg or less
Carbohydrates	54 g	250 g or more
Protein	5 g	55 g to 90 g

WARM BANANA TART

Several components in this special occasion tart provide a rich, complex flavor in every bite. It's layered with a pecan filling, sliced bananas, a broiled custard cream, and served with caramel sauce.

Prep time: 45 minutes plus cooling
Baking time: 33 to 45 minutes
● *Degree of difficulty: challenging*

Pastry
- 1¼ **cups all-purpose flour**
- ½ **cup confectioners' sugar**
  Pinch salt
- 6 **tablespoons cold butter, cut up**
  (no substitutions)
- 1 **large egg, lightly beaten**

Pecan Filling
- 1¼ **cups pecans, ground**
- ½ **cup butter, melted**
  (no substitutions)
- ¼ **cup granulated sugar**
- 1 **large egg**
- ¼ **cup heavy *or* whipping cream**

Pastry Cream
- 1 **cup milk**
- ½ **cup granulated sugar, divided**
- ½ **vanilla bean, split lengthwise, *or***
  1½ teaspoons vanilla extract
- 2 **large egg yolks**
- ¼ **cup all-purpose flour**
- 1 **large, ripe banana, thinly sliced**
- 2 **tablespoons sugar**
  Warm Caramel Sauce
  (recipe at right)

1 For pastry, combine flour, sugar, and salt in a food processor and pulse to combine. Add butter and pulse until mixture resembles fine crumbs. With machine on, add egg through feed tube, processing just until pastry forms a ball. Wrap and refrigerate pastry 1 hour or overnight.

2 On a sheet of lightly floured wax paper, roll pastry into an 11-inch circle. Fit into a 9½-inch tart pan with a removable bottom. Trim pastry overhang to 1 inch from the rim of tart pan then press in against the sides. Prick bottom with a fork. Refrigerate 1 hour or freeze 20 minutes.

3 Preheat oven to 350°F. Bake pastry 20 to 22 minutes or until golden. Cool completely on a wire rack.

4 For pecan filling, combine pecans, butter, sugar, egg, and heavy cream in a medium bowl. Spread evenly over bottom of cooled pastry shell. Bake in the preheated 350°F. oven 15 to 20 minutes or until filling is set. Cool completely on wire rack. (Can be made ahead. Cover and store at room temperature up to 24 hours.)

5 For pastry cream, heat milk, ¼ cup of the sugar, and vanilla bean to boiling in a medium saucepan over medium-high heat. Meanwhile, whisk yolks and remaining ¼ cup sugar in a medium bowl, then whisk in flour until smooth. Gradually whisk in hot milk mixture, then return to saucepan, whisking constantly. Still whisking, bring to a boil. Reduce heat to medium-low and cook, stirring, 1 minute more. Remove from heat and discard vanilla bean. (Stir in vanilla extract, if using.) Transfer to a bowl and cover surface with plastic wrap. Cool, then refrigerate until ready to use. (Can be made ahead. Cover and refrigerate up to 24 hours.)

6 Preheat broiler. Cover edge of tart with a thin strip of foil to prevent burning. Arrange banana slices over cooled pecan filling. Spread an even layer of pastry cream over the fruit, leaving a ½-inch border. Sprinkle cream with the 2 tablespoons sugar. Broil 3 minutes, 4 inches from heat source, or until top is golden brown. Serve tart warm with Warm Caramel Sauce. Makes 12 servings.

PER SERVING
WITHOUT SAUCE

		DAILY GOAL
Calories	390	2,000 (F), 2,500 (M)
Total Fat	25 g	60 g or less (F), 70 g or less (M)
Saturated fat	11 g	20 g or less (F), 23 g or less (M)
Cholesterol	117 mg	300 mg or less
Sodium	172 mg	2,400 mg or less
Carbohydrates	37 g	250 g or more
Protein	5 g	55 g to 90 g

WARM CARAMEL SAUCE

This melt-in-your-mouth dessert sauce is also wonderful over ice cream. It can be prepared ahead, covered and refrigerated up to 24 hours. Gently rewarm over medium heat in a saucepan before serving.

Prep time: 5 minutes
Cooking time: 9 minutes
Degree of difficulty: moderate

¼ **cup butter**
1 **cup granulated sugar**
1 **cup heavy *or* whipping cream**

Melt butter in a medium saucepan over medium-high heat. Add sugar and cook, stirring occasionally, until sugar is melted and mixture is a deep amber color, 6 to 8 minutes. Remove from heat. Gradually stir in cream (mixture will bubble vigorously and be lumpy). Return to heat and cook until sauce is smooth, about 1 minute more. Makes 1⅔ cups.

PER 2 TABLESPOONS

		DAILY GOAL
Calories	155	2,000 (F), 2,500 (M)
Total Fat	10 g	60 g or less (F), 70 g or less (M)
Saturated fat	6 g	20 g or less (F), 23 g or less (M)
Cholesterol	35 mg	300 mg or less
Sodium	43 mg	2,400 mg or less
Carbohydrates	16 g	250 g or more
Protein	0 g	55 g to 90 g

FRESH PEAR AND FIG GALETTES

These free-form French tarts should be served slightly warm or at room temperature—never cold.

Prep time: 1 hour plus chilling
Baking time: 40 minutes
Degree of difficulty: moderate

1½	**cups all-purpose flour**
5½	**teaspoons granulated sugar, divided**
½	**teaspoon salt**
½	**cup plus 2 tablespoons cold butter, cut up (no substitutions)**
6 to 8	**tablespoons ice water**
4	**medium pears, cut into ½-inch slices**
3	**tablespoons fresh lemon juice**
¾	**teaspoon grated lemon peel**
3	**large fresh figs *or* 4 dried, cut into ½-inch slices***
¼	**cup apricot preserves**
1	**tablespoon cognac *or* brandy**

1 For pastry, combine flour, 1½ teaspoons of the sugar, and salt in a medium bowl. Cut in ½ cup of the butter with pastry blender or 2 knives until mixture resembles coarse crumbs. Add water 1 tablespoon at a time, tossing with a fork until pastry comes together. Shape into two thick disks. Wrap in plastic wrap and refrigerate 1 hour or overnight.

2 Preheat oven to 400°F. Toss pear slices with lemon juice and lemon peel in a large bowl; set aside.

3 Grease 2 cookie sheets. On a lightly floured surface, roll 1 pastry disk into an 11-inch circle. Using a 10-inch cake pan or pie plate as a guide, with a small, sharp knife cut a 10-inch pastry circle. Transfer to a prepared cookie sheet. Repeat process with remaining pastry disk.

4 Arrange half the pears along the outside of each pastry circle, overlapping slices and leaving a ½-inch rim. If using fresh figs, arrange half the figs in the center of each circle, staggering and overlapping slices to resemble flower petals. Fold rim up along edge of pears to form a pastry border.

5 Sprinkle each galette with 2 teaspoons of the sugar and dot each with 1 tablespoon of the butter. Bake 40 minutes, switching position of cookie sheets in oven halfway through baking, until crusts are golden and crisp. Immediately transfer galettes to wire rack.

6 For apricot glaze, heat apricot preserves in a small saucepan over medium heat until bubbly. Remove from heat and stir in cognac or brandy. Brush apricot glaze evenly over the top of each warm galette. Serve warm or at room temperature. Makes 12 servings.

***If using dried figs:** After baking galettes 30 minutes, arrange figs as directed above, then bake 10 minutes more.

PER SERVING		DAILY GOAL	
Calories	220	2,000 (F), 2,500 (M)	
Total Fat	10 g	60 g or less (F), 70 g or less (M)	
Saturated fat	6 g	20 g or less (F), 23 g or less (M)	
Cholesterol	28 mg	300 mg or less	
Sodium	199 mg	2,400 mg or less	
Carbohydrates	30 g	250 g or more	
Protein	2 g	55 g to 90 g	

SATIN BERRY TART

Prep time: 1 hour plus chilling
Baking time: 26 to 28 minutes
Degree of difficulty: moderate

- 1¼ **cups all-purpose flour**
- ⅛ **teaspoon salt**
- ½ **cup cold unsalted butter, cut up (no substitutions)**
- 3 **tablespoons ice water**
- 1 **cup milk**
  Half of 1 vanilla bean, split lengthwise
- 3 **large egg yolks**
- ⅓ **cup sugar**
  Pinch salt
- ¼ **cup all-purpose flour**
- 1 **tablespoon unsalted butter (no substitutions)**
- ¼ **cup heavy *or* whipping cream, beaten until stiff**
- 1½ **pints strawberries, halved; raspberries; blueberries; blackberries; *or* a combination**

1 For pastry, combine flour and the ⅛ teaspoon salt in a medium bowl. Gradually add the ½ cup butter, one piece at a time, tossing gently until all pieces are coated with flour. With pastry blender or 2 knives, cut in butter until mixture resembles fine crumbs. Add ice water, 1 tablespoon at a time, tossing vigorously with a fork until pastry just begins to hold together. On a smooth surface, shape pastry into a ball, kneading lightly if necessary. Flatten into a thick disk. Wrap tightly in plastic wrap and refrigerate 1 hour or overnight.

2 Preheat oven to 425°F. On a lightly floured surface, roll pastry into a 14-inch circle, ⅛ inch thick. Carefully transfer to a 9- or 10-inch tart pan with a removable bottom. Press pastry along bottom and up side of pan. With scissors, trim pastry to 1 inch above edge. Fold overhanging pastry in to sides of crust and gently press edge up to extend ¼ inch above side of pan. Prick bottom with a fork. Freeze 20 minutes.

3 Line frozen pastry shell with foil and fill with dried beans or uncooked rice. Bake 12 minutes. Remove foil and beans or rice. Bake pastry 14 to 16 minutes more or until deep golden. Cool completely on a wire rack. Remove sides of pan. Transfer to a serving plate.

4 For custard, bring milk and vanilla bean to a simmer in medium saucepan over medium heat. Remove pan from heat; cover and let stand 10 minutes.

5 Meanwhile, whisk yolks, sugar, and the pinch salt in a medium bowl until pale. Whisk in flour until smooth. Remove vanilla bean and scrape out seeds; return seeds to milk. Gradually whisk hot milk into yolks. Return custard to pan. Bring to a boil over medium heat, whisking constantly; boil gently, whisking, 1 minute. Remove from heat and whisk in the remaining 1 tablespoon butter. Transfer custard to a bowl; cover surface and refrigerate until cold, 2 hours. (Can be made ahead. Cover and refrigerate up to 24 hours.)

6 Before filling tart, whisk custard gently to soften. With a rubber spatula, fold in whipped cream. Spread evenly into baked pastry shell. Arrange fruit over custard. Serve immediately or refrigerate up to 2 hours. Makes 8 servings.

PER SERVING		DAILY GOAL
Calories	320	2,000 (F), 2,500 (M)
Total Fat	19 g	60 g or less (F), 70 g or less (M)
Saturated fat	11 g	20 g or less (F), 23 g or less (M)
Cholesterol	129 mg	300 mg or less
Sodium	74 mg	2,400 mg or less
Carbohydrates	33 g	250 g or more
Protein	5 g	55 g to 90 g

STRAWBERRY-RHUBARB COBBLER

Prep time: 20 minutes
Baking time: 22 to 25 minutes
○ *Degree of difficulty: easy*

- 4 **cups fresh sliced rhubarb**
- 1 **pint strawberries, halved**
- 1 **cup plus 3 tablespoons granulated sugar, divided**
- 2 **tablespoons cornstarch**
- 2 **tablespoons water**
- 1¼ **cups all-purpose flour**
- 1½ **teaspoons baking powder**
- ½ **teaspoon grated lemon peel**
- ⅛ **teaspoon salt**
- ¼ **cup butter *or* margarine, cut up**
- ½ **cup heavy *or* whipping cream, whipped**

1 Preheat oven to 425°F. Combine rhubarb, strawberries, 1 cup of the sugar, cornstarch, and water in a large saucepan. Bring to a boil over medium heat, stirring occasionally. Pour into a 9-inch square baking dish. Set aside and keep hot.

2 Combine flour, 2 tablespoons of the sugar, baking powder, lemon peel, and salt in a bowl. With pastry blender cut in butter until mixture resembles coarse crumbs. Stir in cream until blended. On a lightly floured surface, knead lightly until dough holds together. Roll into an 8-inch square. Place on rhubarb mixture; sprinkle with remaining 1 tablespoon sugar.

3 Place dish on a cookie sheet. Bake 22 to 25 minutes or until golden and bubbly. Serve with whipped cream. Serves 8.

PER SERVING		DAILY GOAL
Calories	320	2,000 (F), 2,500 (M)
Total Fat	12 g	60 g or less (F), 70 g or less (M)
Saturated fat	7 g	20 g or less (F), 23 g or less (M)
Cholesterol	36 mg	300 mg or less
Sodium	182 mg	2,400 mg or less
Carbohydrates	52 g	250 g or more
Protein	3 g	55 g to 90 g

RASPBERRY-PEACH COBBLER

Prep time: 15 minutes
Baking time: 35 minutes
○ *Degree of difficulty: easy*

- 1 **pint raspberries**
- 1 **pound peaches, peeled and sliced**
- ⅔ **cup sugar**
- 1 **tablespoon fresh lemon juice**
- 2 **tablespoons butter *or* margarine**
- 1 **cup all-purpose flour**
- ¼ **cup plus 1 teaspoon sugar, divided**
- ½ **teaspoon baking soda**
- ½ **teaspoon baking powder**
- ⅓ **cup plus 1 tablespoon buttermilk, divided**
- 2 **tablespoons butter *or* margarine, melted**

1 Preheat oven to 400°F. Grease an 8-inch square baking pan. Toss fruit with the ⅔ cup sugar and lemon juice. Spoon into pan; dot with 2 tablespoons butter.

2 Mix flour, the ¼ cup sugar, soda, and baking powder in a bowl. Combine ⅓ cup buttermilk and melted butter. Add to dry ingredients, stirring just until moistened. Shape dough into 2-inch circles about ½ inch thick; place atop fruit.

3 Brush top with remaining 1 tablespoon buttermilk and sprinkle with remaining 1 teaspoon sugar. Bake 35 minutes or until top is golden and bubbly. Serves 6.

PER SERVING		DAILY GOAL
Calories	325	2,000 (F), 2,500 (M)
Total Fat	9 g	60 g or less (F), 70 g or less (M)
Saturated fat	5 g	20 g or less (F), 23 g or less (M)
Cholesterol	23 mg	300 mg or less
Sodium	247 mg	2,400 mg or less
Carbohydrates	59 g	250 g or more
Protein	3 g	55 g to 90 g

FABULOUS

FROZEN DESSERTS

We've packed the best flavors from the deep freeze into this collection of dynamite do-ahead desserts. Our creamiest and easiest homemade ice creams, sorbets and sherbets are hard to beat, especially when you can choose from flavors like Lemon Chiffon, Walnut Brittle, or Mulled Cider. Entertain in style by serving our triple layer Sorbet 'N' Cream Daquoise, Mile-High Frozen Raspberry Ribbon Pie, or luscious Ginger Roll with Frozen Maple Mousse.

SUMMERTIME BLUES-BERRY ICE CREAM

The fresh, uncommon flavor of this frozen berry treat will have your guests begging for seconds!

Prep time: 15 minutes plus chilling and freezing

O *Degree of difficulty: easy*

3 **cups fresh blueberries**
1 **cup granulated sugar**
¼ **cup water**
2 **tablespoons fresh lemon juice**
1 **cup heavy *or* whipping cream**
1 **cup half-and-half cream**

1 Combine blueberries, sugar, and water in a small saucepan. Bring to a boil; cook, stirring, 5 minutes. Puree in batches in a blender until smooth. Transfer to a medium bowl, stir in lemon juice. Refrigerate until cold, 2 hours.

2 Stir heavy cream and half-and-half cream into berry mixture to blend. Transfer to a 2-quart ice cream maker and freeze according to manufacturers' directions.

(Can be made ahead. Spoon into a freezer-proof container. Freeze up to 2 days. Soften in refrigerator 30 minutes before serving.) Makes 6 cups.

PER 1/2 CUP SERVING		DAILY GOAL
Calories	180	2,000 (F), 2,500 (M)
Total Fat	10 g	60 g or less (F), 70 g or less (M)
Saturated fat	6 g	20 g or less (F), 23 g or less (M)
Cholesterol	35 mg	300 mg or less
Sodium	18 mg	2,400 mg or less
Carbohydrates	23 g	250 g or more
Protein	1 g	55 g to 90 g

LEMON CHIFFON ICE CREAM

An ideal summer dessert, this tart, lemony ice cream is a natural with cut-up fruit or berries. Or serve alone with a dollop of our Double Blueberry Sauce (recipe page 76).

Prep time: 15 minutes plus chilling and freezing

O *Degree of difficulty: easy*

4 **cups half-and-half cream**
4 **cups heavy *or* whipping cream**
2 **cups granulated sugar**
4 **teaspoons grated lemon peel**
1 **cup fresh lemon juice**

Heat half-and-half cream, heavy cream, and sugar to boiling in a large saucepan. Remove from heat and stir in lemon peel. Transfer to a bowl; cover and refrigerate overnight. Stir in the lemon juice. Transfer to a 4-quart ice cream maker and freeze according to manufacturers' directions. (Can be made ahead. Spoon into a freezer-proof container. Freeze up to 2 days. Soften in refrigerator 30 minutes before serving.) Makes 2½ quarts.

PER 1/2 CUP SERVING		DAILY GOAL
Calories	305	2,000 (F), 2,500 (M)
Total Fat	23 g	60 g or less (F), 70 g or less (M)
Saturated fat	14 g	20 g or less (F), 23 g or less (M)
Cholesterol	82 mg	300 mg or less
Sodium	38 mg	2,400 mg or less
Carbohydrates	24 g	250 g or more
Protein	2 g	55 g to 90 g

NOTES

_____
_____
_____
_____
_____
_____

WALNUT BRITTLE ICE CREAM

A satiny vanilla custard gives this ice cream an exceptionally smooth texture.

Prep time: 30 to 35 minutes plus chilling and freezing
○ *Degree of difficulty: moderate*

1 **cup sugar, divided**
 Water
 Pinch cream of tartar
½ **cup chopped walnuts**
¼ **cup whole blanched almonds**
6 **large egg yolks**
2 **cups heavy *or* whipping cream**
2 **tablespoons amber rum**
2 **teaspoons vanilla extract**
 Pinch salt

1 Grease a cookie sheet. Combine ½ cup of the sugar, 3 tablespoons water and the cream of tartar in a small saucepan. Cook over medium heat to a deep amber color, 8 to 10 minutes. Stir nuts into caramel. Pour onto prepared cookie sheet and cool completely. Break into pieces. Transfer to a food processor and process until coarsely ground.

2 Heat ¼ cup water and remaining ½ cup sugar to boiling over high heat. Boil, stirring, 2 minutes. Meanwhile, beat egg yolks at high speed in a large mixing bowl until light. Gradually add hot sugar syrup in a slow, steady stream. Continue beating until mixture is thickened and cooled, about 5 minutes.

3 Beat heavy cream in another mixing bowl until stiff; fold into egg mixture with a rubber spatula. Fold in rum, vanilla, and salt just until blended. Refrigerate until cold, 1 hour.

4 Transfer to a 2-quart ice cream maker and freeze according to manufacturers' directions. Stir in brittle and transfer to a freezer-proof container. Freeze until firm, 2 hours or overnight. (Can be made ahead. Spoon into a freezer-proof container. Freeze up to 2 days. Soften in refrigerator 30 minutes before serving.) Makes 1 quart.

PER 1/2 CUP SERVING		DAILY GOAL
Calories	430	2,000 (F), 2,500 (M)
Total Fat	33 g	60 g or less (F), 70 g or less (M)
Saturated fat	15 g	20 g or less (F), 23 g or less (M)
Cholesterol	241 mg	300 mg or less
Sodium	46 mg	2,400 mg or less
Carbohydrates	30 g	250 g or more
Protein	5 g	55 g to 90 g

MAKE MINE VANILLA

This recipe for homemade vanilla ice cream is great with our Almond Butterscotch Sauce (recipe page 76).

Prep time: 5 minutes plus freezing
○ *Degree of difficulty: easy*

2 **cups heavy *or* whipping cream**
2 **cups half-and-half cream**
1 **cup granulated sugar**
1 **teaspoon vanilla extract**

Combine heavy cream, half-and-half cream, and sugar in a medium bowl and stir until sugar is dissolved. Stir in vanilla. Transfer to a 2-quart ice cream maker and freeze according to manufacturers' directions. (Can be made ahead. Spoon into a freezer-proof container. Freeze up to 2 days. Soften in refrigerator 30 minutes before serving.) Makes 6¾ cups.

PER 1/2 CUP SERVING		DAILY GOAL
Calories	225	2,000 (F), 2,500 (M)
Total Fat	17 g	60 g or less (F), 70 g or less (M)
Saturated fat	11 g	20 g or less (F), 23 g or less (M)
Cholesterol	61 mg	300 mg or less
Sodium	28 mg	2,400 mg or less
Carbohydrates	17 g	250 g or more
Protein	2 g	55 g to 90 g

TOFFEE ICE CREAM LAYER CAKE

Tall and handsome, it's easy to assemble and perfect for do-ahead entertaining. Serve alone or with Heavenly Hot Fudge Sauce (recipe, page 76).
Also pictured on the cover.

O *Prep time: 15 minutes plus freezing*
   Baking time: 10 minutes
   Degree of difficulty: easy

 1 **cup (20 cookies) chocolate-wafer crumbs**
 ½ **teaspoon cinnamon**
 2 **tablespoons butter *or* margarine, melted**
 1 **quart premium coffee ice cream**
 3 **bars (1.4 ounces each) chocolate-covered toffee candy, crushed, *or* 1 bag (6 ounces) chocolate-covered toffee candy bits**
 1 **quart premium chocolate ice cream**
 12 **chocolate-wafer cookies, broken up**
 1 **quart premium vanilla ice cream**

1 Preheat oven to 350°F. For crust, combine cookie crumbs and cinnamon in small bowl. Gradually stir in butter until crumbs are moistened. Press into the bottom of a 9-inch springform pan. Bake 10 minutes. Cool completely on wire rack.

2 Refrigerate coffee ice cream to soften slightly, 30 minutes. Quickly spread onto cooled crust and sprinkle with ⅔ cup toffee candy. Freeze until firm, 1 hour.

3 Refrigerate chocolate ice cream to soften slightly, 30 minutes. Quickly spread onto coffee layer and sprinkle top with broken chocolate wafers. Freeze 1 hour. Soften vanilla ice cream as done above. Quickly spread on top of chocolate layer and sprinkle with remaining toffee candy. Cover top and freeze overnight. (Can be made ahead. Wrap well and freeze up to 1 week.)

4 To serve, unwrap cake and refrigerate 20 minutes. Rinse a kitchen towel with warm water and place over the buckle of the side of pan, then remove cake from pan. Makes 12 servings.

PER SERVING		DAILY GOAL
Calories	505	2,000 (F), 2,500 (M)
Total Fat	34 g	60 g or less (F), 70 g or less (M)
Saturated fat	16 g	20 g or less (F), 23 g or less (M)
Cholesterol	93 mg	300 mg or less
Sodium	262 mg	2,400 mg or less
Carbohydrates	47 g	250 g or more
Protein	5 g	5 g to 90 g

ICE CREAM THAT'S A PIECE OF CAKE

Here are some tips on handling ice cream for frozen cakes and pies.

• For desserts with a crust, freeze the crust one hour before assembling or filling your dessert.

• To soften ice cream for filling, remove from freezer and refrigerate 30 minutes for premium brands and 20 minutes for store brands.

• When storing an ice cream dessert, cover the top surface of the ice cream directly with wax paper. Plastic wrap can break when frozen, causing the dessert to dry out or absorb odors.

• Allow the dessert to soften in the refrigerator up to 20 minutes before serving.

CARAMEL CREAM PUFFS WITH CARAMEL ICE CREAM

A luscious triple-caramel treat: cream puffs (French profiteroles) filled with caramel ice cream and topped with a crown of brittle, then sprinkled with praline.

*Prep time: 15 minutes plus cooling,
  chilling and freezing
Baking time: 22 minutes
Degree of difficulty: moderate*

Cream Puffs
- 1 **cup water**
- 6 **tablespoons butter *or* margarine, cut up**
- 1 **tablespoon granulated sugar**
- ⅛ **teaspoon salt**
- 1 **cup all-purpose flour**
- 5 **large eggs**

Brittle Topping
- 1 **cup granulated sugar**
- 2 **tablespoons water**

Caramel Ice Cream
- 1 **cup granulated sugar**
- 2 **tablespoons water**
- 2 **cups heavy *or* whipping cream**
- 1½ **cups milk**
- 4 **large egg yolks**
  Pinch salt

Praline
- 2 **teaspoons vegetable oil**
- ¾ **cup granulated sugar**
- 1 **cup pecans, chopped**

1 Preheat oven to 425° F. For cream puffs, grease 2 cookie sheets. Bring water, butter, sugar, and salt to a boil in a large saucepan until butter is melted. Remove from heat. Add flour all at once and beat vigorously with a wooden spoon until smooth. Cook, stirring, over medium heat until pastry pulls away from sides of pan, about 1 minute.

2 Transfer pastry to a large mixing bowl. Beat 30 seconds to cool slightly. At medium speed, add eggs one at a time, beating well after each addition.

3 Spoon into a large pastry bag fitted with a ½-inch plain tip and pipe 1½-inch mounds 1½ inches apart on prepared cookie sheets. Bake 22 minutes, rotating pans once, until golden. Cool.

4 For brittle topping, combine sugar and water in a medium saucepan. Cook over medium-high heat, stirring with a wooden spoon just until sugar dissolves. Bring to a boil without stirring. Cook to a deep amber color. Remove pan from heat and carefully place in a bowl of cool water for 30 seconds.

5 Place puffs on wire racks over a sheet of wax paper. Carefully spoon brittle topping evenly over tops. Cool 10 minutes.

6 For caramel ice cream, combine sugar and water in a medium saucepan. Cook over medium-high heat, stirring with a wooden spoon just until sugar dissolves. Then bring to a boil without stirring. Cook to a deep amber color. Carefully stir in cream and milk (mixture will bubble vigorously). Return to heat, stirring, until mixture is smooth.

7 Meanwhile, whisk egg yolks and salt in a large bowl. Gradually whisk in half the hot cream mixture. Return to saucepan with remaining cream. Cook, stirring constantly, over medium heat until mixture coats the back of a spoon, 4 minutes. Strain through a fine sieve into a clean bowl. Cover and refrigerate until completely cold, 3 hours. (Can be made ahead. Refrigerate up to 24 hours.)

8 Transfer custard to an ice cream maker and freeze according to manufacturers' directions. Spoon into a freezer-proof container; cover and freeze overnight.

9 Cut each puff in half horizontally. Spoon about 2 tablespoons caramel ice cream and replace top. Cover and freeze up to 2 hours. Arrange 3 puffs on each dessert plate. Sprinkle with chopped praline. Makes 14 servings.

Praline: Oil a cookie sheet using the vegetable oil. Place sugar in a small saucepan. Cook over medium-high heat, stirring with a wooden spoon just until sugar dissolves. Bring to a boil without stirring. Cook to a deep amber color. Remove from heat and stir in nuts. Pour onto prepared cookie sheet and cool completely. Transfer praline to a cutting board and coarsely chop. Makes 1½ cups.

PER 3 PUFFS; 1/2 CUP ICE CREAM, 1 TABLE-SPOON PRALINE

		DAILY GOAL
Calories	460	2,000 (F), 2,500 (M)
Total Fat	28 g	60 g or less (F), 70 g or less (M)
Saturated fat	14 g	20 g or less (F), 23 g or less (M)
Cholesterol	219 mg	300 mg or less
Sodium	136 mg	2,400 mg or less
Carbohydrates	48 g	250 g or more
Protein	6 g	55 g to 90 g

FROZEN STRAWBERRY MARGARITA DESSERT

This tequila-spiked sensation is pure refreshment for the summertime crowd after a spicy meal or barbeque.

Prep time: 45 minutes plus freezing
Degree of difficulty: moderate

1 **package (16 ounces) frozen, whole strawberries, thawed**
⅓ **cup tequila**
2 **tablespoons fresh lime juice**
1 **cup sugar**
1 **teaspoon unflavored gelatin**
⅔ **cup water**
1 **tablespoon light corn syrup**
2 **large egg whites**
  Pinch salt
1 **cup heavy *or* whipping cream**
  Fresh strawberry halves, for garnish

1 Puree thawed strawberries, tequila, and lime juice in a food processor until smooth.

2 Combine sugar and gelatin in a small saucepan. Stir in water and corn syrup and let stand 1 minute to soften gelatin. Cook over medium-high heat until syrup reaches soft-ball stage (234°F. to 240°F.) on a candy thermometer. Meanwhile, beat egg whites and salt in a large mixing bowl on medium-high speed until stiff but not dry. Add hot syrup in a thin, steady stream, beating constantly, until mixture is completely cool, about 5 minutes. Fold in strawberry mixture with a rubber spatula.

3 Beat cream in another mixing bowl to soft peaks. Fold into strawberry mixture. Spoon half the mixture into a 2-quart glass serving dish. Arrange fresh strawberry halves, cut side facing out, around inside of glass dish. Spoon in remaining strawberry mixture, smoothing top. Cover and freeze overnight. (Can be made ahead. Wrap well and freeze up to 2 weeks.) Let stand at room temperature 15 minutes before serving. Makes 2 quarts.

PER 1/2 CUP SERVING		DAILY GOAL
Calories	130	2,000 (F), 2,500 (M)
Total Fat	6 g	60 g or less (F), 70 g or less (M)
Saturated fat	3 g	20 g or less (F), 23 g or less (M)
Cholesterol	20 mg	300 mg or less
Sodium	22 mg	2,400 mg or less
Carbohydrates	17 g	250 g or more
Protein	1 g	55 g to 90 g

FROZEN RASPBERRY RIBBON PIE

We make the most of the ruby red raspberry, by layering a rich berry puree with vanilla ice cream, all under a gorgeous meringue bonnet.

Ⓜ️ *Microwave*
Prep time: 40 minutes plus freezing
Degree of difficulty: easy

○

1½ **cups (30 cookies) chocolate-wafer crumbs**
¼ **cup butter *or* margarine, melted**
2 **cups fresh raspberries**
½ **cup granulated sugar**
1 **tablespoon cornstarch**
¼ **cup butter *or* margarine, cut up**
2 **pints premium vanilla ice cream**
4 **large egg whites, at room temperature**
Pinch salt
⅓ **cup granulated sugar**
½ **teaspoon vanilla extract**

1 For crust, preheat oven to 350°F. Combine cookie crumbs and the melted butter in a small bowl until crumbs are evenly moistened. Press into the bottom and up the sides of a 9-inch pie pan. Bake 10 minutes. Cool completely on wire rack, then freeze crust 1 hour.

2 For filling, puree raspberries in a food processor or blender, then strain through a fine sieve into a 4-cup microwave-proof measure. Stir in the ½ cup sugar and cornstarch; add the ¼ cup butter. Cover with plastic wrap, turning back one section to vent. Microwave on high (100% power), stirring once, until thickened, about 4 minutes. Whisk until smooth, then cool to room temperature.

3 Refrigerate 1 pint ice cream to soften slightly, 30 minutes. Quickly spread evenly over crust and cover with 1 cup raspberry puree. Freeze 30 minutes. Repeat layering process with remaining 1 pint ice cream and raspberry puree. Freeze 30 minutes. Cover pie and freeze overnight.

4 Preheat oven to 450°F. For topping, beat egg whites and salt in a large mixing bowl at medium speed until soft peaks form. Gradually beat in the ⅓ cup sugar and vanilla, and continue to beat at medium speed to stiff peaks.

5 Unwrap frozen pie. With a spatula, spread meringue completely over top of pie, mounding more meringue in center. Swirl through meringue with back of a spoon to form decorative peaks. Bake until topping is browned, about 2 minutes. Immediately place in freezer and freeze at least 1 hour. (Can be made ahead. Cover and freeze up to 2 days.) Makes 12 servings.

PER SERVING		DAILY GOAL	
Calories	290	2,000 (F), 2,500 (M)	
Total Fat	14 g	60 g or less (F), 70 g or less (M)	
Saturated fat	8 g	20 g or less (F), 23 g or less (M)	
Cholesterol	40 mg	300 mg or less	
Sodium	224 mg	2,400 mg or less	
Carbohydrates	37 g	250 g or more	
Protein	4 g	55 g to 90 g	

NOTES

_____

_____

_____

_____

_____

_____

EASY ICE CREAM TOPPERS

Enjoy your homemade ice cream, sherbet or sorbet with any of these super sundae sauces.

Heavenly Hot Fudge Sauce: Combine 4 squares (4 ounces) unsweetened chocolate, coarsely chopped, and ⅔ cup heavy *or* whipping cream in a 1-quart microwave-proof bowl. Microwave on high (100% power) 1½ minutes. Stir until chocolate is completely melted. Stir in ⅔ cup granulated sugar. Microwave 1 minute more. Stir to dissolve sugar, then stir in 2 tablespoons butter and 1 teaspoon vanilla extract until smooth. Serve warm. (Can be made ahead. Cool. Cover and refrigerate up to 3 days. Microwave on high (100% power) 1½ to 2 minutes, stirring after 1 minute, until warm and smooth.) Makes 1⅔ cups.

Per 1 tablespoon: 70 calories, 5 g total fat, 3 g saturated fat, 11 mg cholesterol, 12 mg sodium, 7 g carbohydrates, 1 g protein.

Raspberry-Peach Sauce: Combine 1½ cups diced fresh peaches *or* nectarines (2 medium), 1 tablespoon granulated sugar, and 1 teaspoon fresh lemon juice in a medium bowl. Let stand 10 minutes. Combine ½ cup raspberries and ¼ cup light corn syrup in a blender and puree until smooth. Add to peaches. Makes 1¾ cups.

Per 2 tablespoons: 30 calories, 0 g total fat, 0 g saturated fat, 0 mg cholesterol, 8 mg sodium, 8 g carbohydrates, 0 g protein.

Double Blueberry Sauce: Combine 1 cup fresh blueberries, ⅓ cup granulated sugar, 2 tablespoons cold water, and 1½ teaspoons cornstarch in a small saucepan. Bring to a boil, stirring occasionally. Then reduce heat and simmer 1 minute. Remove from heat and stir in 1 more cup blueberries and 1 teaspoon fresh lemon juice. Makes 1½ cups.

Per ¼ cup: 70 calories, 0 g total fat, 0 g saturated fat, 0 mg cholesterol, 3 mg sodium, 18 g carbohydrates, 0 g protein.

Almond Butterscotch Sauce: Melt 1 tablespoon butter in a medium saucepan over medium heat. Add ¼ cup chopped almonds and cook, stirring, until golden. Stir in ½ cup packed brown sugar, ⅓ cup light corn syrup, and ¼ cup heavy *or* whipping cream. Reduce heat to medium-low and boil, stirring, 3 minutes. Remove from heat and stir in 2 tablespoons amaretto liqueur. Serve warm. Makes 1½ cups.

Per tablespoon: 55 calories, 3 g total fat, 1 g saturated fat, 5 mg cholesterol, 14 mg sodium, 7 g carbohydrates, 4 g protein.

EASIEST FRUIT SORBETS

Luscious fruit sorbets are a true summer treat, and what's more, you don't need any special equipment to make them. Just freeze some plums, peaches, or honeydew, puree with a simple sugar syrup in the food processor and grab a spoon! You can keep the frozen fruit and syrup up to three days, and whip up a batch whenever you crave a cool snack or easy low-fat dessert.

▼   *Low-fat*
▽   *Low-calorie*
    Prep time: 15 minutes plus chilling
○   *and freezing*
    Degree of difficulty: easy

1 **pound peeled peaches *or* unpeeled plums, pitted and cut into 1-inch chunks *or* 3½ cups chopped honeydew**
⅓ **cup granulated sugar**
⅔ **cup water**
1 **teaspoon fresh lemon juice (optional)**

1 Line a cookie sheet with wax paper and arrange desired cut fruit in a single layer. Freeze until firm, at least 2 hours.

2 Meanwhile, heat sugar and water in a small saucepan to boiling then reduce heat and simmer 1 minute or until sugar is dissolved. Refrigerate until syrup is cold, at least 2 hours.

3 Remove fruit from freezer and let stand 3 minutes. Place in food processor and pulse until coarsely chopped. With machine on, add syrup in a slow, steady stream and process until sorbet is smooth. Add lemon juice if desired. Spoon into a 1-quart freezer-proof container and freeze 30 minutes or until ready to serve. (Can be made ahead. Freeze up to 2 days. Soften in refrigerator 15 minutes before serving.) Makes 2½ cups peach and plum sorbet, 3¼ cups honeydew sorbet.

PER 1/2 CUP PEACH SORBET		DAILY GOAL
Calories	80	2,000 (F), 2,500 (M)
Total Fat	0 g	60 g or less (F), 70 g or less (M)
Saturated fat	0 g	20 g or less (F), 23 g or less (M)
Cholesterol	0 g	300 mg or less
Sodium	0 mg	2,400 mg or less
Carbohydrates	21 g	250 g or more
Protein	0 g	55 g to 90 g

PER 1/2 CUP PLUM SORBET		DAILY GOAL
Calories	100	2,000 (F), 2,500 (M)
Total Fat	0 g	60 g or less (F), 70 g or less (M)
Saturated fat	0 g	20 g or less (F), 23 g or less (M)
Cholesterol	0 g	300 mg or less
Sodium	0 mg	2,400 mg or less
Carbohydrates	24 g	250 g or more
Protein	1 g	55 g to 90 g

PER 1/2 CUP HONEYDEW SORBET		DAILY GOAL
Calories	75	2,000 (F), 2,500 (M)
Total Fat	0 g	60 g or less (F), 70 g or less (M)
Saturated fat	0 g	20 g or less (F), 23 g or less (M)
Cholesterol	0 g	300 mg or less
Sodium	10 mg	2,400 mg or less
Carbohydrates	20 g	250 g or more
Protein	0 g	55 g to 90 g

MEET YOUR MAKER
Always chill your ice cream, sherbet, or sorbet mixture in the refrigerator before adding it to your ice cream maker.

GINGER ROLL WITH FROZEN MAPLE MOUSSE

Prep time: 1 hour plus freezing
Baking time: 17 to 18 minutes
Degree of difficulty: moderate

¼ **cup all-purpose flour**
¼ **cup cornstarch**
½ **teaspoon cinnamon**
½ **teaspoon ginger**
   Pinch cloves
4 **large eggs, at room temperature, separated**
¾ **cup granulated sugar, divided**
   Pinch salt
⅛ **teaspoon cream of tartar**
   Sifted confectioners' sugar
¾ **cup pure maple syrup (no substitutions)**
2 **large egg whites**
1 **cup heavy *or* whipping cream Unsweetened cocoa and maple syrup, for garnish**

1 Preheat oven to 350° F. For ginger roll, grease a 15½x10½-inch jelly-roll pan. Line with wax paper and grease paper. Sift flour, cornstarch, cinnamon, ginger, and cloves in a medium bowl and set aside.

2 Beat egg yolks and ¼ cup of the sugar at high speed in a large mixing bowl until a ribbon forms when beaters are lifted, 3 minutes. With clean beaters, beat egg whites and salt in another larger mixing bowl at medium speed until foamy. Add cream of tartar and continue to beat to soft peaks. Gradually increasing speed to high, beat in remaining ½ cup sugar, 1 tablespoon at a time, until egg whites are stiff.

3 Fold one-fourth of egg white mixture into yolk mixture with a rubber spatula. Fold in dry ingredients alternately with remaining meringue until just blended. Spread batter evenly in prepared pan. Bake 17 to 18 minutes, or until cake springs back when lightly touched in center.

4 Meanwhile, place a clean kitchen towel on a work surface and sprinkle generously with sifted confectioners' sugar. Invert cake onto towel, remove jelly-roll pan and carefully peel off paper. Roll up cake from one long side, transfer to a wire rack and cool completely, seam side down.

5 For maple mousse, bring maple syrup to a boil in a small saucepan over medium-low heat. Cook until syrup reaches thread stage (225°F.-230F.) on a candy thermometer.

6 Meanwhile, beat egg whites and a pinch of salt in a large mixing bowl at medium speed until stiff. With mixer on, add hot syrup in a thin, steady stream. Increase speed to high and beat 5 minutes more or until mixture is cool. In another large mixing bowl, beat cream until stiff, then fold into maple mixture with a rubber spatula.

7 To assemble, line a cookie sheet with wax paper. Unroll cake and carefully transfer to prepared cookie sheet. Spread top with an even layer of maple mousse. Freeze flat until filling is semi-firm, 1 hour. Re-roll cake into a log. Freeze, seam side down, 2 hours. (Can be made ahead. Wrap and freeze up to 2 days.)

8 To serve, sift cocoa onto 8 dessert plates. Cut cake into 16 slices. Arrange 2 slices on each plate and drizzle with maple syrup. Makes 8 servings.

PER SERVING		DAILY GOAL	
Calories	325	2,000 (F), 2,500 (M)	
Total Fat	14 g	60 g or less (F), 70 g or less (M)	
Saturated fat	8 g	20 g or less (F), 23 g or less (M)	
Cholesterol	147 mg	300 mg or less	
Sodium	93 mg	2,400 mg or less	
Carbohydrates	47 g	250 g or more	
Protein	5 g	55 g to 90 g	

SORBET 'N' CREAM DACQUOISE

Prep time: 1 hour plus cooling, chilling, and freezing
Baking time: 2 to 2½ hours
● *Degree of difficulty: moderate*

- **7 large egg whites, at room temperature**
- **¼ teaspoon cream of tartar**
- **1½ cups granulated sugar**
- **2 teaspoons vanilla extract**
- **¼ cup plus 2 tablespoons confectioners' sugar, divided**
- **2 pints premium chocolate ice cream**
- **1 cup blanched almonds, toasted and ground**
- **1 pint raspberry sorbet**
- **2 squares (2 ounces) semisweet chocolate, chopped**
- **1¼ cups heavy *or* whipping cream, divided**
- **Fresh raspberries, for garnish**

1 Preheat oven to 225°F. Line 2 large cookie sheets with parchment paper and draw two 8-inch squares on each sheet.

2 Beat egg whites in a large mixing bowl at medium speed until frothy. Add cream of tartar; beat to soft peaks. Gradually increase speed to high and beat in granulated sugar 1 tablespoon at a time. Beat 1 minute more, then beat in vanilla. Sift ¼ cup of the confectioners' sugar over egg whites and gently fold together with a rubber spatula just until blended.

3 Spoon half the meringue into a large pastry bag fitted with a large plain tip. Pipe meringue in close parallel lines filling the 2 squares on one prepared cookie sheet. Repeat process with remaining meringue for remaining 2 squares. Bake 2 to 2½ hours, or until meringues are dry to the touch, switching cookie sheets halfway through. Cool on pans 5 minutes, then carefully transfer to wire racks with a wide metal spatula. Cool completely.

4 Place one meringue smooth side down on a serving plate. Refrigerate 1 pint each chocolate ice cream and sorbet to soften slightly, 20 minutes. Gently spread chocolate ice cream over meringue and sprinkle with one-third of the almonds. Top with second meringue and press down gently. Quickly spread sorbet over top and sprinkle with another third of nuts. Top

with third meringue and freeze until firm, about 30 minutes.

5 Meanwhile, soften remaining 1 pint chocolate ice cream. Spread over third meringue and sprinkle with remaining nuts. Top with fourth meringue smooth side down. Freeze until firm, 2 hours. Heat chocolate and ¼ cup of the cream in a small saucepan over low heat stirring until smooth. Drizzle over top meringue layer and freeze overnight. (Can be made ahead. Freeze until chocolate is hardened, 1 hour. Wrap well and freeze up to 1 week.)

6 Beat remaining 1 cup cream with remaining 2 tablespoons confectioners' sugar until stiff. Spoon 1 cup into a pastry bag fitted with a star tip. With a thin metal spatula, spread remaining cream over sides of cake. Pipe cream decoratively on top edge. Freeze until cream is firm, 1 hour or up to 24 hours. Garnish with raspberries just before serving. Makes 16 servings.

PER SERVING		DAILY GOAL	
Calories	310	2,000 (F), 2,500 (M)	
Total Fat	15 g	60 g or less (F), 70 g or less (M)	
Saturated fat	7 g	20 g or less (F), 23 g or less (M)	
Cholesterol	37 mg	300 mg or less	
Sodium	60 mg	2,400 mg or less	
Carbohydrates	42 g	250 g or more	
Protein	5 g	55 g to 90 g	

MULLED CIDER SORBET

Spice-infused frozen apple cider with a splash of sweet port wine makes for a most unusual and refreshing sorbet.

▼ *Low-fat*
Prep time: 10 minutes plus standing and freezing
○ *Degree of difficulty: easy*

1 **cup port wine**
¾ **cup granulated sugar**
3 **strips (3 inches each) orange peel**
2 **cinnamon sticks**
5 **whole cloves**
4 **cups apple cider**

1 Combine port, sugar, orange peel, cinnamon, and cloves in a small saucepan. Bring to a boil over high heat, stirring to dissolve sugar, 3 minutes. Cool to room temperature.

2 Strain port mixture through a fine sieve into a large bowl. Stir in the cider. Transfer mixture to an ice cream maker and freeze according to manufacturers' directions.

(Can be made ahead. Transfer to a freezer-proof container and freeze up to 3 days.) Makes 5½ cups.

PER 1/2 CUP SERVING		DAILY GOAL
Calories	130	2,000 (F), 2,500 (M)
Total Fat	0 g	60 g or less (F), 70 g or less (M)
Saturated fat	0 g	20 g or less (F), 23 g or less (M)
Cholesterol	0 mg	300 mg or less
Sodium	5 mg	2,400 mg or less
Carbohydrates	27 g	250 g or more
Protein	0 g	55 g to 90 g

TROPICAL SHERBET

Four ingredients are all you need for this sherbet that tastes like paradise. If your supermarket carries frozen mango puree, you can use it, but you'll still need to puree the ingredients in the blender.

Prep time: 10 minutes plus chilling and freezing
○ *Degree of difficulty: easy*

1 **large mango, peeled, pitted, cut into 1-inch chunks (about 1¼ cups)**
1 **can (15 ounces) cream of coconut**
1 **cup water**
6 **tablespoons fresh lime juice**

Combine mango and cream of coconut in a blender and puree until smooth. Add water and lime juice; blend on low speed until combined. Transfer to a bowl and refrigerate until cold, about 1 hour. Transfer mixture to an ice cream maker and freeze according to manufacturers' instructions. (Can be made ahead. Spoon into a freezer-proof container. Freeze up to 2 days. Soften in refrigerator 30 minutes before serving.) Makes 5 cups.

PER 1/2 CUP SERVING		DAILY GOAL
Calories	120	2,000 (F), 2,500 (M)
Total Fat	10 g	60 g or less (F), 70 g or less (M)
Saturated fat	9 g	20 g or less (F), 23 g or less (M)
Cholesterol	0 mg	300 mg or less
Sodium	28 mg	2,400 mg or less
Carbohydrates	9 g	250 g or more
Protein	2 g	55 g to 90 g

NOTES

_____

_____

_____

_____

_____

_____

_____

CRANBERRY-RASPBERRY SORBET WITH PEAR CHIPS

This sorbet is rich in color, flavor and texture—and delightfully low in fat. Use an adjustable-blade vegetable slicer to cut the thinnest pear slices for this unusual fruit garnish. *Also pictured on page 66.*

▼   *Low-fat*
▽   *Low- calorie*
   Prep time: 15 minutes plus chilling and freezing
   Baking time: 5 to 8 minutes per batch
○   *Degree of difficulty: easy*

1   **bag (12 ounces) fresh *or* frozen and thawed cranberries**
   Water
1   **cup granulated sugar**
½   **cup light corn syrup**
1   **bag (12 ounces) frozen whole raspberries, thawed**

Pear Chips
2   **teaspoons vegetable oil**
1   **firm Bosc *or* Bartlett pear**
2   **teaspoons granulated sugar**

1   For sorbet, heat cranberries, 1 cup water and the 1 cup sugar in a large saucepan. Cook until cranberries begin to soften, 3 minutes. Remove from heat. Add ½ cup water, corn syrup, and raspberries. Puree mixture in batches in a food processor or blender until smooth. Strain through a fine sieve into a bowl. Cover and refrigerate until cold, about 3 hours or overnight.

2   Transfer mixture to an ice cream maker and freeze according to manufacturers' directions. Spoon into freezer-proof container and freeze until firm. (Can be made ahead. Freeze up to 2 days. Soften in refrigerator 15 minutes before serving.) Serve with Pear Chips. Makes 7 cups.

Pear Chips: Preheat oven to 375°F. Brush 2 cookie sheets with the oil; set aside. Slice pear lengthwise very thinly with an adjustable-blade slicer.* Arrange slices in a single layer on prepared sheets. Sprinkle with sugar. Bake in batches until golden and crisp, 5 to 8 minutes. Remove any golden chips and continue baking

remaining chips. Cool chips on wire racks. Store in an airtight container. (If necessary, re-crisp the chips in a 375°F. oven 2 to 3 minutes.) Makes about 4 dozen.

*Adjustable-blade vegetable slicers (mandolines) are available in cookware shops and by mail from Katagiri & Co., 212-838-5453.

PER 1/2 CUP WITH 3 CHIPS		DAILY GOAL
Calories	130	2,000 (F), 2,500 (M)
Total Fat	1 g	60 g or less (F), 70 g or less (M)
Saturated fat	0 g	20 g or less (F), 23 g or less (M)
Cholesterol	0 mg	300 mg or less
Sodium	15 mg	2,400 mg or less
Carbohydrates	32 g	250 g or more
Protein	0 g	55 g to 90 g

NOTES

_____

_____

_____

_____

_____

_____

_____

_____

CLASSIC CAKES

AND

CHEESECAKES

Naturally, cake is part of our dessert collection, and here's a selection of old favorites and new delights. Plunge into Citrus Chiffon Cake, Ambrosia Layer Cake, or Cinnamon Angel Food Cake—each one is a mile high and lighter than air. Or savor every crumb of confections like Double Almond or spicy Black Pepper Pound Cakes. And don't forget the ultimate indulgence: cheesecake. We've got glorious Blueberry Swirl for fruit lovers, and a Triple Layer Cheesecake with creamy vanilla, espresso, and chocolate layers for the dessert love in all of us!

BLUEBERRY SWIRL CHEESECAKE

You'll get a refreshing bite of berry in each creamy slice of this glorious cheesecake.

Prep time: 30 minutes plus chilling
Baking time: 1¼ hours
⬤ *Degree of difficulty: moderate*

1½ **cups blueberries**
1¼ **cup plus 2 tablespoons granulated sugar, divided**
2 **teaspoons cornstarch**
1 **tablespoon fresh lemon juice**
1 **cup graham cracker cookie crumbs**
2 **tablespoons butter *or* margarine, melted**
3 **packages (8 ounces each) cream cheese *or* Neufchâtel cheese, at room temperature**
1 **container (8 ounces) sour cream**
2 **teaspoons vanilla extract**
4 **large eggs, at room temperature**
2 **tablespoons all-purpose flour**

1 For blueberry puree, combine blueberries, ¼ cup of the sugar, and cornstarch in a medium saucepan. Bring to a boil over medium heat and cook, stirring, 5 minutes. Puree in blender with lemon juice. Cool completely.

2 Preheat oven to 350° F. For crust, combine cookie crumbs, 2 tablespoons of the sugar, and butter in small bowl until crumbs are evenly moistened. Pat crumbs evenly over the bottom of a 9-inch springform pan. Bake 10 minutes. Cool on wire rack. Keep oven on. Tightly cover bottom and sides of springform pan with heavy-duty foil.

3 For filling, beat cream cheese in large mixing bowl at medium-high speed until light and fluffy, 2 minutes. Gradually beat in the remaining 1 cup sugar, scraping sides of bowl with a rubber spatula, until mixture is completely smooth, 3 minutes. Beat in sour cream and vanilla. With mixer at low speed, add eggs 1 at a time, beating just until blended after each addition. Beat in flour just until combined.

4 Pour filling over crust in pan and place in a large roasting pan. Carefully drizzle blueberry puree over batter. Swirl a thin knife through batter to marbleize. Place pan on oven rack. Carefully pour enough boiling water into roasting pan to come 1 inch up side of springform pan. Bake 1¼ hours or until center is just set. Turn oven off; let the cheesecake stand in oven 1 hour.

5 Remove cheesecake from water bath. Cool completely on wire rack. Remove foil. Cover and refrigerate overnight. Just before serving, run a knife around edge of pan and remove sides. Makes 12 servings.

PER SERVING		DAILY GOAL	
Calories	430	2,000 (F), 2,500 (M)	
Total Fat	28 g	60 g or less (F), 70 g or less (M)	
Saturated fat	17 g	20 g or less (F), 23 g or less (M)	
Cholesterol	147 mg	300 mg or less	
Sodium	280 mg	2,400 mg or less	
Carbohydrates	37 g	250 g or more	
Protein	8 g	55 g to 90 g	

NOTES

_____

_____

_____

_____

_____

_____

TRIPLE LAYER CHEESECAKE

The key to making the distinct coffee, chocolate, and vanilla layers is freezing the cheesecake after adding each flavor, then baking.

Prep time: 45 minutes plus freezing and chilling
Baking time: 1½ hours
Degree of difficulty: moderate

- ¾ **cup chocolate wafer cookie crumbs**
- 1 **tablespoon butter *or* margarine, melted**
- 4 **packages (8 ounces each) cream cheese *or* Neufchâtel cheese, at room temperature**
- 1¾ **cups granulated sugar**
- 1 **teaspoon vanilla extract**
  Pinch salt
- 4 **large eggs, at room temperature**
- 1 **teaspoon instant espresso powder**
- 1 **tablespoon hot water**
- 3 **squares (3 ounces) unsweetened chocolate, melted and cooled**

1 Preheat oven to 350ª F. For crust, butter an 8-inch springform pan. Combine cookie crumbs and butter in a small bowl until crumbs are evenly moistened. Pat crumbs evenly over bottom of prepared pan. Bake 10 minutes. Cool on wire rack. Tightly cover bottom and sides of springform pan with heavy-duty foil.

2 Meanwhile, for filling, beat cream cheese in large mixing bowl at medium-high speed until light and fluffy, 2 minutes. Gradually beat in sugar, scraping sides of bowl with a rubber spatula, until mixture is completely smooth, 3 minutes. Reduce speed to medium and beat in vanilla and salt. Add eggs 1 at a time, beating just until blended after each addition.

3 Dissolve espresso powder in hot water. Place 2 cups cream cheese filling in a medium bowl and fold in espresso with a rubber spatula. Pour over crust in pan and freeze until firm, about 1½ hours.

4 Place another 1¾ cups cream cheese filling in a medium bowl and fold in melted chocolate. Carefully spread over coffee layer and freeze 20 minutes.

5 Preheat oven to 350°F. Spread remaining cream cheese filling over chocolate layer; place springform pan in a large roasting pan. Place pan on oven rack. Carefully pour enough hot water into roasting pan to come 1 inch up side of springform pan. Bake 1½ hours or until center is just set.

6 Remove cheesecake from water bath. Cool completely on wire rack. Remove foil. Cover and refrigerate overnight. Just before serving, run a knife around edge of pan and remove sides. Makes 12 servings.

PER SERVING		DAILY GOAL	
Calories	480	2,000 (F), 2,500 (M)	
Total Fat	34 g	60 g or less (F), 70 g or less (M)	
Saturated fat	20 g	20 g or less (F), 23 g or less (M)	
Cholesterol	158 mg	300 mg or less	
Sodium	311 mg	2,400 mg or less	
Carbohydrates	38 g	250 g or more	
Protein	9 g	55 g to 90 g	

NOTES

_____

_____

_____

_____

_____

_____

VERY BERRY CHEESECAKE

The lemony blend of cream cheese, cottage cheese, and sour cream makes this cheesecake filling extra-light in texture. *Also pictured on page 84.*

Prep time: 25 minutes plus chilling
Baking time: 1¼ hours
Degree of difficulty: moderate

¾ **cup graham cracker cookie crumbs**
¼ **cup finely chopped walnuts**
1 **tablespoon firmly packed brown sugar**
2 **tablespoons butter *or* margarine, melted**
1 **container (8 ounces) cream-style cottage cheese**
2 **packages (8 ounces each) cream cheese *or* Neufchâtel cheese, at room temperature**
1¼ **cups granulated sugar**
1 **tablespoon fresh lemon juice**
1 **teaspoon vanilla extract**
½ **teaspoon grated lemon peel**
   Pinch salt
4 **large eggs, at room temperature**

1 **container (8 ounces) sour cream**
   Fresh strawberries, blueberries, and raspberries, for garnish
Double Strawberry Sauce
2 **packages (10 ounces each) frozen strawberries in light syrup, thawed**
1 **pint fresh strawberries, thinly sliced**

1 Preheat oven to 350° F. For crust, butter an 8-inch springform pan. Combine cookie crumbs, walnuts, brown sugar, and butter in a small bowl until crumbs are evenly moistened. Pat crumbs evenly over bottom of prepared pan. Bake 10 minutes. Cool on wire rack. Keep oven on. Tightly cover bottom and sides of springform pan with heavy-duty foil.

2 Meanwhile, for filling, puree cottage cheese in food processor or blender until smooth. Beat cream cheese in large mixing bowl at medium-high speed until light and fluffy, 2 minutes. Beat in cottage cheese. Gradually beat in sugar, scraping sides of bowl with a rubber spatula, until mixture is completely smooth, 3 minutes. Reduce speed to medium. Beat in lemon juice, vanilla, lemon peel, and salt. Add eggs, 1 at

a time, beating just until blended after each addition. Beat in sour cream just until smooth.

3 Pour filling over crust in pan and place in a large roasting pan. Place pan on oven rack. Carefully pour enough hot water into roasting pan to come 1 inch up side of springform pan. Bake 1¼ hours or until center is just set.

4 Remove cheesecake from water bath. Cool completely on wire rack. Remove foil. Cover and refrigerate overnight. Just before serving, run knife around edge of pan and remove sides. Serve with Double Strawberry Sauce. Garnish top with fresh berries. Makes 12 servings.

Double Strawberry Sauce: Puree strawberries in syrup in food processor or blender until smooth. Transfer to a medium bowl and stir in sliced strawberries. Makes 3⅓ cups.

PER SERVING WITH 1/4 CUP SAUCE		DAILY GOAL
Calories	420	2,000 (F), 2,500 (M)
Total Fat	24 g	60 g or less (F), 70 g or less (M)
Saturated fat	13 g	20 g or less (F), 23 g or less (M)
Cholesterol	130 mg	300 mg or less
Sodium	301 mg	2,400 mg or less
Carbohydrates	45 g	250 g or more
Protein	9 g	55 g to 90 g

PASSION FRUIT CHEESECAKE

If you love tropical flavors, seek out fresh passion fruit. The purplish egg-shaped variety gives one to two tablespoons of juice. The larger, yellow-green variety yields three to four tablespoons.

Prep time: 30 minutes plus chilling
Baking time: 70 minutes
Degree of difficulty: moderate

- ¾ **cup vanilla wafer cookie crumbs**
- ¼ **cup blanched slivered almonds, toasted and finely chopped**
- 2 **tablespoons butter *or* margarine, melted**
- 4 **packages (8 ounces each) cream cheese *or* Neufchâtel cheese, at room temperature**
- 1¾ **cups granulated sugar**
- ½ **cup fresh *or* frozen passion fruit juice, thawed***
- 2 **teaspoons vanilla extract**
  Pinch salt
- 4 **large eggs, at room temperature**
  Sliced mango, for garnish

1 Preheat oven to 350° F. For crust, butter a 9-inch springform pan. Combine cookie crumbs and almonds in a small bowl. Stir in butter until crumbs are evenly moistened. Pat crumbs evenly over bottom of prepared pan. Bake 10 minutes. Cool on wire rack. Keep oven on. Tightly cover the bottom and sides of springform pan with heavy-duty foil.

2 Meanwhile, for filling, beat cream cheese in large mixing bowl at medium-high speed until light and fluffy, 2 minutes. Gradually beat in sugar, scraping sides of bowl with a rubber spatula, until mixture is completely smooth, 3 minutes. Reduce speed to medium and beat in passion fruit juice, vanilla, and salt. Add eggs 1 at a time, beating just until blended after each addition.

3 Pour filling over crust in pan and place in a large roasting pan. Place pan on oven rack. Carefully pour enough boiling water into roasting pan to come 1 inch up side of springform pan. Bake 1 hour 10 minutes minutes or until center is just set.

4 Remove cheesecake from water bath. Cool completely on wire rack. Remove foil. Cover and refrigerate overnight. Just before serving, run a knife around edge of pan and remove sides. Makes 12 servings.

*Frozen passion fruit puree is available in Asian and Spanish specialty groceries. For fresh juice, cut 8 passion fruit in half and scoop out pulp and seeds with a spoon. Transfer to a fine sieve set over a small bowl; strain pulp through sieve, pressing with back of spoon. Discard seeds.

PER SERVING		DAILY GOAL
Calories	475	2,000 (F), 2,500 (M)
Total Fat	33 g	60 g or less (F), 70 g or less (M)
Saturated fat	19 g	20 g or less (F), 23 g or less (M)
Cholesterol	162 mg	300 mg or less
Sodium	297 mg	2,400 mg or less
Carbohydrates	39 g	250 g or more
Protein	9 g	55 g to 90 g

NOTES

CHEESECAKE SUCCESS

Nothing is more magical than a perfect slice of luscious cheesecake. And mastering your cheesecake-making technique is easy. Here are some hints:

Buttery Crumb Crust: The easiest crust around. Be creative and use your favorite crushed cookie crumbs. Be sure to thoroughly cool the crust after baking; this will keep it moist but not soggy.

Creaming that Cream Cheese: Whether you use regular cream cheese or Neufchâtel, be sure the cheese is thoroughly softened at room temperature. We do not recommend whipped cream cheese; it will affect the volume and density of your cake.

Beat the cream cheese in a large mixing bowl at medium-high speed until creamy, at least 2 minutes. Gradually add the sugar, a spoonful at a time, frequently scraping the sides of the mixing bowl with a rubber spatula, until thoroughly combined. Beat 3 minutes longer until very light, fluffy, and completely smooth. This method of beating ensures the cake will have a smooth texture.

The Best Blend: When adding the remaining ingredients, it's crucial to reduce your mixer speed to medium. When adding the room temperature eggs and additional liquid ingredients or flavorings, beat just until blended after each addition.

Hot Water Bath: The best method for a creamy cheesecake that is less likely to sink or crack is to bake it in a hot-water bath, also called a bain-marie. Covering the outside of your springform pan with heavy-duty foil or a double layer of foil forms a strong seal and prevents leaking. Add your filling to the springform pan and then place the pan in a larger pan (we use a large roasting pan) and pour in enough boiling water to come 1 inch up the side of the smaller pan. The hot water helps distribute the heat evenly during baking. Your cheesecake will be creamy and light every time.

Freezing: Cool the cheesecake to room temperature as directed. Wrap the pan well with plastic wrap and freeze up to 1 month. Thaw in the refrigerator overnight before serving.

FRESH GINGER CHEESECAKE

True fresh ginger fans might want to add another teaspoon of grated ginger, but taste the batter first! This cheesecake is delectable with sliced fresh peaches, nectarines, or apricots.

Prep time: 25 minutes plus chilling
Baking time: 1¼ hours
Degree of difficulty: moderate

1	**cup gingersnap cookie crumbs**
2	**tablespoons butter** *or* **margarine, melted**
3	**packages (8 ounces each) cream cheese** *or* **Neufchâtel cheese, at room temperature**
1½	**cups granulated sugar**
1	**tablespoon freshly grated ginger**
1	**teaspoon fresh lemon juice**
1	**teaspoon vanilla extract**
	Pinch salt
4	**large eggs, at room temperature**
⅓	**cup heavy** *or* **whipping cream**

1 Preheat oven to 350° F. For crust, butter an 8-inch springform pan. Combine cookie crumbs and butter in small bowl until crumbs are evenly moistened. Pat crumbs evenly over bottom of prepared pan. Bake 10 minutes. Cool on wire rack. Keep oven on. Tightly cover bottom and sides of springform pan with heavy-duty foil.

2 Meanwhile, for filling, beat cream cheese in large mixing bowl at medium-high speed until light and fluffy, 2 minutes. Gradually beat in sugar, scraping sides of bowl with a rubber spatula, until mixture is completely smooth, 3 minutes. Reduce speed to medium and beat in ginger, lemon juice, vanilla, and salt. Add eggs 1 at a time, beating just until blended after each addition. Add cream and beat just until blended.

3 Pour filling over crust in pan and place in a large roasting pan. Place pan on oven rack. Carefully pour enough hot water into roasting pan to come 1 inch up side of springform pan. Bake 1¼ hours or until center is just set.

4 Remove cheesecake from water bath. Cool completely on wire rack. Remove foil.

Cover and refrigerate overnight. Just before serving, run a knife around edge of pan and remove sides. Makes 12 servings.

PER SERVING		DAILY GOAL
Calories	410	2,000 (F), 2,500 (M)
Total Fat	28 g	60 g or less (F), 70 g or less (M)
Saturated fat	17 g	20 g or less (F), 23 g or less (M)
Cholesterol	156 mg	300 mg or less
Sodium	274 mg	2,400 mg or less
Carbohydrates	34 g	250 g or more
Protein	7 g	55 g to 90 g

NOTES

_____

_____

_____

_____

_____

_____

_____

_____

_____

_____

_____

_____

_____

NO BAKE ALMOND-RICOTTA CHEESECAKE

This delicious amaretto-flavored cheesecake in a double chocolate wafer crust is simple to make.

Ⓜ *Microwave*
Prep time: 20 minutes plus chilling
Ⓞ *Degree of difficulty: easy*

- 2 **squares (2 ounces) semisweet chocolate, melted and cooled**
- 1 **cup (20 cookies) chocolate wafer cookie crumbs**
- 1 **envelope unflavored gelatin**
- 3 **tablespoons amaretto liqueur**
- 1 **tablespoon cold water**
- 1 **cup heavy *or* whipping cream**
- ¾ **cup granulated sugar**
- 2 **containers (15 ounces each) ricotta cheese**
  Chocolate shavings, for garnish

1 For crust, combine melted chocolate and cookie crumbs in a small bowl. Press evenly over bottom of an 8- or 9-inch springform pan. Freeze until ready to use.

2 Sprinkle gelatin over amaretto and water in a 1-cup microwave-proof measure. Let stand 2 minutes to soften. Microwave on high (100% power) 40 seconds; stir. In another microwave-proof measure, microwave cream on high (100% power) 45 seconds, until hot. Transfer hot cream to a blender. With machine on, add gelatin through the hole in lid and blend until gelatin is completely dissolved, about 1 minute. Scrape down sides of blender and blend again. Add sugar and blend until dissolved. Add 1 container ricotta, blend until smooth. Transfer half the mixture to a large bowl. Add the remaining container ricotta to blender and blend until smooth. Stir into the mixture in the bowl.

3 Pour batter into prepared pan. Cover and refrigerate at least 8 hours. Just before serving, run a small knife around edge of pan and remove sides. Garnish top with chocolate shavings. Makes 12 servings.

PER SERVING		DAILY GOAL
Calories	315	2,000 (F), 2,500 (M)
Total Fat	19 g	60 g or less (F), 70 g or less (M)
Saturated fat	11 g	20 g or less (F), 23 g or less (M)
Cholesterol	63 mg	300 mg or less
Sodium	127 mg	2,400 mg or less
Carbohydrates	25 g	250 g or more
Protein	10 g	55 g to 90 g

CITRUS CHIFFON CAKE

This light-as-air classic cake is a perfect springtime treat. It travels beautifully and is terrific with fresh fruit. The recipe calls for cake flour, and it's worth buying. Store any unused flour in the freezer.

Prep time: 15 minutes plus cooling
Baking time: 55 to 60 minutes
○ *Degree of difficulty: easy*

2¼ **cups sifted cake flour**
      (not self-rising flour)
1½ **cups granulated sugar**
1   **tablespoon baking powder**
1   **teaspoon salt**
½   **cup vegetable oil**
5   **large egg yolks, at room**
      temperature
1   **tablespoon grated orange peel**
2   **teaspoons grated lemon peel**
¾   **cup fresh orange juice**
8   **large egg whites, at room**
      temperature
½   **teaspoon cream of tartar**
1   **tablespoon confectioners' sugar**

1 Preheat oven to 325°F. Sift flour, sugar, baking powder, and salt into a large bowl. Make a wide well in center. Add oil, then egg yolks, orange peel, lemon peel, and orange juice. Whisk until smooth; set aside.

2 Beat all the egg whites in a large mixing bowl at medium speed until frothy. Add cream of tartar. Gradually increasing speed, continue beating to stiff peaks. Gradually pour yolk mixture in a thin, steady stream into beaten whites, folding gently with a rubber spatula.

3 Pour batter into an ungreased 10-inch tube pan. Bake 55 to 60 minutes or until toothpick inserted halfway between tube and side of pan comes out clean and cake springs back when touched gently. Immediately invert pan onto neck of funnel or bottle; let hang until completely cool, about 3 hours.

4 To loosen, run a metal spatula or thin knife around side of pan and tube. Invert pan again and remove cake. Turn cake upright onto serving plate. Sprinkle top with sifted confectioners' sugar. Makes 16 servings.

PER SERVING		DAILY GOAL
Calories	220	2,000 (F), 2,500 (M)
Total Fat	8 g	60 g or less (F), 70 g or less (M)
Saturated fat	1 g	20 g or less (F), 23 g or less (M)
Cholesterol	67 mg	300 mg or less
Sodium	260 mg	2,400 mg or less
Carbohydrates	32 g	250 g or more
Protein	4 g	55 g to 90 g

NOTES

_____
_____
_____
_____
_____
_____
_____
_____
_____
_____
_____
_____
_____

CINNAMON ANGEL CAKE WITH ORANGE COMPOTE

Our favorite low-fat angel food cake is spiced up with cloves and cinnamon and served with a fresh orange compote.

Prep time: 1 hour plus cooling
Baking time: 35 to 40 minutes
Degree of difficulty: moderate

1   **cup cake flour**
1½ **cups granulated sugar, divided**
1   **teaspoon cinnamon**
   Pinch cloves
12 **large egg whites, at room temperature**
1½ **teaspoons cream of tartar**
½   **teaspoon salt**
1¼ **teaspoons grated orange peel**
1   **cup confectioners' sugar, sifted**
1½ **teaspoons dark rum**
1   **to 2 tablespoons fresh orange juice**

Orange Compote
8   **navel oranges**
1   **cup water**
½   **cup granulated sugar**
1   **tablespoon orange-flavored liqueur**

1 Preheat oven to 375°F. Sift flour, ¾ cup of the granulated sugar, cinnamon, and cloves together 3 times; set aside. Beat egg whites in a large mixing bowl until foamy, 4 minutes. Gradually increasing speed to medium, add cream of tartar and salt. Add the remaining ¾ cup sugar, 1 tablespoon at a time, beating well after each addition. Beat at medium speed until mixture holds stiff peaks when beaters are lifted, 2 minutes. Beat in 1 teaspoon of the orange peel.

2 Sift one-third of the dry ingredients over the beaten whites; carefully fold in with a rubber spatula. Repeat twice more with remaining dry ingredients just until blended.

3 Pour batter into an ungreased 10-inch tube pan. Cut through batter with a knife or metal spatula to remove any air pockets. Bake 35 to 40 minutes, until top of cake springs back when pressed with fingertip.

4 Immediately invert pan onto funnel or bottle; let stand until completely cool. Run a knife around side of pan and tube to unmold cake. Transfer to a serving plate.

5 For glaze, combine confectioners' sugar, rum, remaining ¼ teaspoon orange peel, and juice in a small bowl. Add remaining juice as needed to make a thick glaze. Drizzle over cake. Serve with Orange Compote. Makes 10 servings.

Orange Compote: Peel 1 orange with a vegetable peeler; cut peel into julienne. Bring water and sugar to a boil in a medium saucepan; add peel and boil 2 minutes. Remove from heat. With a sharp knife, cut peel and white pith from remaining oranges; cut between membranes to remove sections. Combine orange sections, any juice that has collected, and liqueur. Makes 5 cups.

PER SERVING		DAILY GOAL	
Calories	320	2,000 (F), 2,500 (M)	
Total Fat	0 g	60 g or less (F), 70 g or less (M)	
Saturated fat	0 g	20 g or less (F), 23 g or less (M)	
Cholesterol	0 mg	300 mg or less	
Sodium	177 mg	2,400 mg or less	
Carbohydrates	75 g	250 g or more	
Protein	6 g	55 g to 90 g	

RASPBERRY-ORANGE CAKE ROLL

This elegant version of the classic jelly-roll has two fillings, a vibrant fruit puree and a liqueur-spiked whipped cream studded with fresh berries.

Prep time: 30 minutes plus chilling
Baking time: 10 to 12 minutes
Degree of difficulty: moderate

- ⅓ **cup all-purpose flour**
- ⅓ **cup cornstarch**
- ½ **teaspoon salt**
- 5 **large eggs, separated, at room temperature**
- ½ **cup plus 2 tablespoons granulated sugar, divided**
- 1 **teaspoon grated orange peel**
- 1 **teaspoon vanilla extract**
  Confectioners' sugar
- 1 **pint raspberries, divided**
- 1 **teaspoon unflavored gelatin**
- 1 **tablespoon water**
- 1 **tablespoon raspberry-flavored brandy**
- 1 **cup heavy *or* whipping cream**

1 Preheat oven to 375°F. Grease a 15½x10½-inch jelly-roll pan. Line with wax paper. Grease and flour paper; tap to remove excess flour. Sift flour, cornstarch, and salt together. Beat egg whites in a large mixing bowl at medium speed until frothy. Gradually beat in ½ cup of the granulated sugar until stiff but not dry; set aside.

2 Beat egg yolks in a clean mixing bowl at medium-high speed until pale and thick, 3 minutes. Add orange peel and vanilla. Gently fold in beaten whites with a rubber spatula. Fold in dry ingredients just until blended (*do not overmix*). Spread batter evenly in prepared pan. Bake 10 to 12 minutes or until lightly browned and cake springs back when lightly touched in center.

3 Sift confectioners' sugar lightly over a clean kitchen towel. Invert hot cake onto towel, remove pan and peel off paper. Roll towel and cake up together from one long side. Let stand 1 minute, then unroll cake to let steam escape. Re-roll with towel and place on a wire rack seam side down to cool completely.

4 For filling, puree ½ pint raspberries in a food processor or blender. Strain through a fine sieve into a small bowl. Stir in remaining 2 tablespoons granulated sugar and set aside.

5 Sprinkle gelatin over water in a small saucepan and let stand 2 minutes to soften. Cook, stirring, over low heat until gelatin is dissolved. Stir in brandy. Beat cream, ⅓ cup confectioners' sugar, and gelatin mixture in a large mixing bowl to stiff peaks. Reserving a few raspberries for garnish, fold remaining berries into cream mixture.

6 Unroll cake and spread raspberry puree to within 1 inch of edge. Spread cream mixture over puree. Roll up and place cake seam side down on a serving platter; trim ends of roll with a serrated knife. Sprinkle top with additional confectioners' sugar. Garnish with reserved raspberries. Refrigerate 30 minutes before serving. Makes 12 servings.

PER SERVING		DAILY GOAL
Calories	200	2,000 (F), 2,500 (M)
Total Fat	10 g	60 g or less (F), 70 g or less (M)
Saturated fat	6 g	20 g or less (F), 23 g or less (M)
Cholesterol	126 mg	300 mg or less
Sodium	140 mg	2,400 mg or less
Carbohydrates	22 g	250 g or more
Protein	4 g	55 g to 90 g

COFFEE-HAZELNUT BÛCHE DE NOËL

Inspired by the classic French Christmas cake, we filled a sponge-nut roll with a special coffee buttercream that gets its flavor from heating milk with espresso.

Prep time: 1½ hours plus chilling
Baking time: 15 to 17 minutes
Degree of difficulty: challenging

¼ **cup hazelnuts, toasted and skinned (see tip, page 122)**
1½ **cups granulated sugar, divided**
4 **large eggs, separated, at room temperature, plus 4 egg yolks**
1 **teaspoon vanilla extract**
¼ **teaspoon salt**
¾ **cup all-purpose flour**
   Confectioners' sugar
¾ **cup milk**
2 **tablespoons ground espresso coffee**

4 **large egg yolks**
1 **tablespoon coffee liqueur**
1 **cup unsalted butter (no substitutions)**
4 **squares (4 ounces) semisweet chocolate, melted**
¼ **cup brewed espresso coffee, cooled**
1 **tablespoon hazelnut-flavored liqueur**

1 Preheat oven to 350°F. Grease a 15½x10½-inch jelly-roll pan. Line with wax paper. Grease and flour paper; tap to remove excess flour.

2 In a food processor, process hazelnuts with ¼ cup of the granulated sugar until finely ground. Beat 4 egg yolks with ¼ cup of the sugar in a large mixing bowl at high speed until mixture is pale and thick and forms a ribbon when beaters are lifted, 3 minutes. Beat in vanilla and salt. Beat egg whites in a clean mixing bowl at medium speed until frothy. Gradually add ¼ cup of the sugar and continue to beat until stiff. Gently fold beaten whites into yolks with a rubber spatula. Sift flour over top and fold in just until blended. Fold in hazelnut mixture.

3 Spread batter evenly in prepared pan and bake 15 to 17 minutes or until cake springs back when lightly touched in center. Sift confectioners' sugar lightly over a clean kitchen towel. Invert hot cake onto towel, remove pan and peel off paper. Roll towel and cake up together from one long side. Place on a wire rack seam-side down to cool completely.

4 For coffee buttercream, bring milk to a boil in a small saucepan. Remove from heat and stir in ground coffee. Let stand 20 minutes. Strain through a fine sieve lined with a double layer of cheesecloth into a clean medium saucepan; discard coffee grounds. Reheat milk to simmering over medium heat.

5 Meanwhile, whisk remaining 4 yolks with remaining ¾ cup sugar in a medium bowl. Gradually whisk in hot milk. Return mixture to saucepan and cook, stirring constantly, over medium-low heat until mixture thickens slightly and coats the back of a spoon *(do not boil)*. Strain through a sieve into a mixing bowl. Stir in coffee liqueur. Cool to room temperature. Beat in butter, 1 tablespoon at a time, beating well after each addition. (If mixture appears curdled, let stand at room temperature 15 minutes, then beat again at high speed until smooth and silky. If mixture appears oily, refrigerate 15 minutes then beat at high speed until smooth.)

6 Line a cookie sheet with parchment or wax paper. Spread melted chocolate on paper to a 10x8-inch rectangle. Refrigerate until firm.

7 To assemble, unroll cake. Combine brewed espresso with hazelnut liqueur and brush evenly over inside of cake with a pastry brush. Reserve ½ cup buttercream for ends. Spread half of the remaining buttercream on top of cake and reroll. Place cake seam-side down on a cookie sheet and frost the outside with remaining half of buttercream.

8 With a sharp knife, cut off a piece diagonally about 2 inches from end of the log to make the branch stump. Attach branch stump to top of log. Frost exposed ends of cake with reserved ½ cup buttercream and draw a ring pattern with tines of a fork.

9 Break cooled chocolate into 1-inch-wide strips by bending paper. Press strips onto buttercream to form bark. Cover loosely with plastic wrap and refrigerate up to 24 hours. One hour before serving, remove cake from refrigerator and transfer to a serving platter with a large spatula. Slice with a serrated knife. Makes 12 servings.

PER SERVING		DAILY GOAL
Calories	396	2,000 (F), 2,500 (M)
Total Fat	25 g	60 g or less (F), 70 g or less (M)
Saturated fat	13 g	20 g or less (F), 23 g or less (M)
Cholesterol	187 mg	300 mg or less
Sodium	85 mg	2,400 mg or less
Carbohydrates	40 g	250 g or more
Protein	5 g	55 g to 90 g

OUR BEST DEVIL'S FOOD CAKE

This triple-layer chocolate cake with a creamy fudge frosting is pure comfort. The cocoa-sour cream combo and the secret ingredient—coffee—add depth of flavor and a dark, rich color.

Prep time: 40 minutes plus cooling
Baking time: 25 minutes
Degree of difficulty: moderate

- ¾ **cup milk**
- 2 **teaspoons instant coffee powder**
- ¾ **cup unsweetened cocoa**
- ½ **cup sour cream**
- 1¼ **cups all-purpose flour**
- 1½ **teaspoons baking soda**
- ½ **teaspoon baking powder**
  Pinch salt
- 1 **cup butter, softened (no substitutions)**
- 1½ **cups granulated sugar**
- 3 **large eggs, at room temperature**
- 2 **teaspoons vanilla extract**

Creamy Fudge Frosting
- 4 **squares (4 ounces) unsweetened chocolate, coarsely chopped**
- 1⅔ **cups confectioners' sugar**
- ¾ **cup heavy or whipping cream**
- 2 **teaspoons vanilla extract**
- 6 **tablespoons butter, softened, cut up (no substitutions)**

1 Preheat oven to 350°F. Butter three 8-inch round cake pans. Line bottoms with wax paper. Butter and flour paper; tap to remove excess flour.

2 Heat milk and coffee in small saucepan over medium heat until small bubbles form around edge. Add cocoa and whisk until smooth. Whisk in sour cream. Cool.

3 Combine flour, baking soda, baking powder, and salt in a medium bowl. Beat butter in a large mixing bowl at medium speed until light. Gradually beat in sugar until light and fluffy. Beat in eggs, 1 at a time, beating well after each addition. Add vanilla. At low speed, gradually beat in dry ingredients, alternately with chocolate mixture, beginning and ending with dry ingredients. Beat at medium speed 2 minutes. Pour into prepared pans.

4 Bake 25 minutes or until tops spring back when lightly touched. Cool in pans on wire racks 10 minutes. Invert cakes onto racks. Carefully peel off wax paper, then cool completely, right side up.

5 Place 1 layer on cake plate and spread with ¾ cup Creamy Fudge Frosting. Top with second layer and another ¾ cup frosting. Top with third layer and spread top and sides with remaining frosting. Makes 12 servings.

Creamy Fudge Frosting: Heat chocolate, confectioners' sugar, and heavy cream, stirring constantly, in medium saucepan over medium heat until smooth. Remove from heat; stir in vanilla. Transfer to a large mixing bowl, and place in a larger bowl of ice water. Let stand, stirring occasionally, until cold and thick. Remove from ice bath. Gradually beat in butter at high speed; beat until frosting is fluffy and stiff enough to hold its shape.

PER SERVING		DAILY GOAL
Calories	570	2,000 (F), 2,500 (M)
Total Fat	37 g	60 g or less (F), 70 g or less (M)
Saturated fat	22 g	20 g or less (F), 23 g or less (M)
Cholesterol	139 mg	300 mg or less
Sodium	391 mg	2,400 mg or less
Carbohydrates	59 g	250 g or more
Protein	6 g	55 g to 90 g

DOUBLE ALMOND POUND CAKE

This dense, rich cake prepared with almond paste and a candy-like topping is easy to make, travels well, and freezes beautifully. To serve, thaw completely, then before serving crisp it briefly in a 300° F. oven for a just-baked taste.

Prep time: 20 minutes plus cooling
Baking time: 45 to 50 minutes
○ *Degree of difficulty: moderate*

½ **cup blanched slivered almonds**
1⅓ **cups granulated sugar**
¼ **cup unsalted butter**
  (no substitutions)
1 **tablespoon milk**
1½ **cups plus 1 tablespoon all-purpose**
  flour, divided
½ **teaspoon cream of tartar**
½ **teaspoon salt**
¾ **cup unsalted butter, softened**
  (no substitutions)
⅓ **cup almond paste**
4 **large eggs, at room temperature**
1 **tablespoon fresh lemon juice**
1 **teaspoon grated lemon peel**
1 **teaspoon vanilla extract**
  Sweetened whipped cream and
  raspberries, for garnish

1 For topping, combine almonds, ⅓ cup of the sugar, the ¼ cup butter, and milk in a small saucepan and heat over low heat until butter is melted. Set aside.

2 Preheat oven to 350°F. Butter and flour a 9-inch springform pan. Combine 1½ cups of the flour with cream of tartar and salt in a medium bowl. Beat the ¾ cup softened butter and the almond paste in a large mixing bowl on medium-high speed until creamy. Gradually add the remaining 1 cup sugar and continue beating until light and fluffy and completely smooth, about 5 minutes. Beat in eggs 1 at a time, beating a minute after each addition. Stir in lemon juice, lemon peel, and vanilla. Add dry ingredients and beat 1 minute more. Pour into prepared pan and smooth top. Sprinkle evenly with remaining 1 tablespoon flour and spoon topping evenly over top.

3 Bake 40 to 50 minutes or until toothpick inserted in center comes out clean. Cool completely in pan on a wire rack. (Can be made ahead. Wrap well and store at room temperature up to 2 days or freeze up to 1 month.) Remove springform sides of pan. Serve with sweetened whipped cream and raspberries. Makes 12 servings.

PER SERVING (WITHOUT CREAM OR BERRIES)		DAILY GOAL
Calories	370	2,000 (F), 2,500 (M)
Total Fat	22 g	60 g or less (F), 70 g or less (M)
Saturated fat	11 g	20 g or less (F), 23 g or less (M)
Cholesterol	112 mg	300 mg or less
Sodium	117 mg	2,400 mg or less
Carbohydrates	39 g	250 g or more
Protein	6 g	55 g to 90 g

NOTES

_____

_____

_____

_____

_____

_____

_____

_____

_____

BLACK PEPPER POUND CAKE

This old-fashioned spice cake will become one of your tea time favorites. Wrap well and let stand overnight, then cut into thin slices for serving.

Prep time: 30 minutes plus standing
Baking time: 1 hour
O *Degree of difficulty: Moderate*

1½   **cups all-purpose flour**
½   **teaspoon cream of tartar**
½   **teaspoon salt**
½   **teaspoon freshly ground pepper**
¼   **teaspoon mace *or* nutmeg**
1   **cup unsalted butter, softened**
     (no substitutions)
1   **cup granulated sugar**
4   **large eggs, at room temperature**
1   **tablespoon fresh lemon juice**
1   **teaspoon vanilla extract**

1 Preheat oven to 325°F. Butter and flour a 6-cup kugelhopf or bundt pan; tap to remove excess flour.

2 Combine flour, cream of tartar, and salt in a medium bowl. Beat butter in a large mixing bowl on medium-high speed until creamy. Gradually add sugar and continue beating until light and fluffy, about 5 minutes. Beat in eggs 1 at a time, beating a minute after each addition. Stir in lemon juice and vanilla. Add dry ingredients and beat 1 minute more. Pour into prepared pan.

3 Bake 1 hour or until toothpick inserted in center comes out clean. Cool in pan on a wire rack 15 minutes, then remove from pan and cool completely. Wrap well and let stand overnight. Makes 16 servings.

PER SERVING		DAILY GOAL
Calories	220	2,000 (F), 2,500 (M)
Total Fat	13 g	60 g or less (F), 70 g or less (M)
Saturated fat	8 g	20 g or less (F), 23 g or less (M)
Cholesterol	85 mg	300 mg or less
Sodium	90 mg	2,400 mg or less
Carbohydrates	22 g	250 g or more
Protein	3 g	55 g to 90 g

NOTES

103

CAKE SENSE

Do you wonder why your cakes aren't light and fluffy? The secret of a light butter cake is to cream the butter and sugar properly.

Creaming: Always start with softened butter. Beat in a large mixing bowl 30 seconds until creamy at medium-high speed. Gradually add the sugar, a spoonful at a time, scraping the sides of the mixing bowl with a rubber spatula. Beat 4 to 5 minutes longer until very light and fluffy. This method of beating ensures the cake will have a smooth texture and rise properly.

Adding the eggs: Eggs at room temperature blend with the other ingredients more easily. Remove them from the refrigerator 1 hour before using or place them (in the shell) in a bowl of warm water 10 minutes. On low speed, add the eggs to the creamed butter mixture 1 at a time, beating 1 minute after each addition.

Adding the dry ingredients: This should be done at low speed. Add the dry ingredients just until blended. (Do not overmix the batter or your cake will be tough.) If adding dry ingredients with a liquid, begin and end with the dry ingredients.

Doneness: When a toothpick inserted in center of cake comes out clean, the top is golden, and the cake begins to come away from the sides of the pan, it's done.

A Fast Frost Fix: To easily frost a layer cake, place a layer on a serving plate. Tuck 4 strips of wax paper under the cake. For a double layer cake, spread the bottom layer with one-third of the frosting (for a triple layer, spread the bottom and middle layers with one-fourth of the frosting each). Add remaining cake layer and frost top and sides of cake with remaining frosting. Remove strips of wax paper.

WARM APPLE SPICE CAKE

Granny Smith apples offer a tart contrast to the sweet, spicy cake. Served warm with a caramel sauce, this dessert is super satisfying.

Ⓜ *Microwave*
  Prep time: 30 minutes plus cooling
  Baking time: 1 hour 10 minutes
⬤ *Degree of difficulty: moderate*

2½ cups peeled, chopped Granny Smith apples
2 cups all-purpose flour
1½ teaspoons baking powder
½ teaspoon baking soda
¼ teaspoon salt
1 teaspoon cinnamon
½ teaspoon ginger
¼ teaspoon cloves
¼ teaspoon nutmeg
¾ cup butter *or* margarine, softened
½ cup granulated sugar
½ cup firmly packed brown sugar
3 large eggs

½ **cup milk**
½ **cup chopped walnuts**
½ **cup dark raisins**
1 **Granny Smith apple, peeled and sliced thin**
2 **tablespoons confectioners' sugar**
¼ **cup apple jelly, heated**
  Warm Caramel Sauce
  (recipe page 61)

1 Preheat oven to 350°F. Butter a 9x3-inch springform pan. Line bottom of pan with wax paper; butter paper.

2 Place apples in a microwave-proof dish. Cover and microwave on high (100% power) 3 to 4 minutes or until soft. Mash with the back of a spoon. Cool completely.

3 Combine flour, baking powder, baking soda, salt, cinnamon, ginger, cloves, and nutmeg in a bowl; set aside. Beat butter, granulated sugar, and brown sugar in a large mixing bowl at medium speed until light and fluffy. Add eggs 1 at a time, beating well after each addition. At low speed, beat in dry ingredients alternately with milk. Fold in chopped apples, nuts, and raisins. Spoon batter into prepared

pan; smooth top. Arrange apple slices in a circle along outside edge . Bake 1 hour 10 minutes or until toothpick inserted in center comes out clean. Cool slightly on a wire rack.

4 To unmold, run a knife around sides of springform pan, remove, then invert cake. Peel off wax paper and invert again onto serving plate. Sprinkle cake with confectioners' sugar, then brush apple slices with melted jelly. Serve warm with Warm Caramel Sauce. Makes 10 servings.

PER SERVING

WITHOUT SAUCE		DAILY GOAL
Calories	435	2,000 (F), 2,500 (M)
Total Fat	20 g	60 g or less (F), 70 g or less (M)
Saturated fat	10 g	20 g or less (F), 23 g or less (M)
Cholesterol	103 mg	300 mg or less
Sodium	370 mg	2,400 mg or less
Carbohydrates	60 g	250 g or more
Protein	6 g	55 g to 90 g

NOTES

105

AMBROSIA LAYER CAKE

This orange and coconut cake recalls the classic fruit compote, ambrosia, a holiday-time tradition at the Southern table.

Prep time: 45 minutes plus cooling
Baking time: 25 minutes
Degree of difficulty: moderate

2¾ cups sifted cake flour
2 teaspoons baking powder
¾ teaspoon salt
10 tablespoons unsalted butter, softened (no substitutions)
2¼ cups granulated sugar, divided
3 large eggs, at room temperature
1¼ cups milk
1½ teaspoons vanilla extract
1¼ cups fresh orange juice
5 large egg yolks
10 tablespoons cold unsalted butter, cut up (no substitutions)
4 teaspoons fresh lemon juice
1 teaspoon grated orange peel
1½ cups heavy *or* whipping cream
3 tablespoons confectioners' sugar
⅓ cup cream of coconut
1 tablespoon dark rum
1 cup unsweetened coconut chips* or flaked coconut

1 For cake, preheat oven to 350°F. Butter three 8-inch round cake pans. Line bottoms with wax paper. Butter and flour paper; tap to remove excess flour.

2 Combine flour, baking powder, and salt in a medium bowl. Beat softened butter and 1¾ cups of the granulated sugar in a large mixing bowl until light and fluffy. Add eggs 1 at a time, beating 1 minute after each addition. Combine milk and vanilla and add to batter, alternating with dry ingredients at low speed, beginning and ending with dry ingredients. Beat at medium speed 2 minutes until completely smooth. Pour into prepared pans.

3 Bake 25 minutes or until cakes pull away from sides of pans and tops spring back when touched lightly. Cool in pans on wire racks 10 minutes. Invert cakes onto racks. Carefully peel off wax paper then cool completely, right side up.

4 For orange filling, bring orange juice to boil in a small saucepan over high heat; boil until reduced to ⅓ cup. Combine yolks, cold butter, the remaining ½ cup granulated sugar, and lemon juice in a medium saucepan. Add reduced orange juice and cook, stirring, over medium-low heat until butter is melted and custard coats the back of a spoon, about 10 minutes *(do not boil)*. Transfer to a small bowl and stir in orange peel. Cover surface with plastic wrap and refrigerate until cold, 1 hour.

5 With a serrated knife, cut each cake in half horizontally. Place a cake layer, cut side up, on a serving plate and spread with scant ⅓ cup orange filling on top. Repeat, stacking 4 more cake layers and remaining orange filling, ending with remaining cake layer, cut side down. (Can be made ahead. Wrap well and refrigerate up to 24 hours.)

6 Beat cream in a large mixing bowl to soft peaks. Add confectioners' sugar and continue beating until stiff. Beat in cream of coconut and rum. Spread whipped cream over top and sides of cake. Decorate sides of cake with coconut chips. Refrigerate up to 4 hours. Makes 16 servings.

*Coconut chips are unsweetened coconut shavings available in health food stores and Asian markets.

PER SERVING		DAILY GOAL
Calories	475	2,000 (F), 2,500 (M)
Total Fat	30 g	60 g or less (F), 70 g or less (M)
Saturated fat	19 g	20 g or less (F), 23 g or less (M)
Cholesterol	178 mg	300 mg or less
Sodium	195 mg	2,400 mg or less
Carbohydrates	45 g	250 g or more
Protein	5 g	55 g to 90 g

RYE BREAD TORTE

Don't let the name throw you! In the 19th century, bread was often used in Europe to intensify the flavor of cakes. Jenifer Harvey Lang shared her husband's favorite recipe with us.

Prep time: 24 minutes plus cooling
Baking time: 30 minutes
Degree of difficulty: moderate

1   cup seedless rye bread crumbs
1   cup walnuts, ground
1   teaspoon baking powder
6   large eggs, at room temperature,
        separated
    Pinch salt
1   cup granulated sugar

2   cups heavy *or* whipping cream
1   teaspoon cinnamon
1   teaspoon vanilla extract
1   jar (12 ounces) seedless raspberry
        jam

1   Preheat oven to 375°F. Butter three 9-inch round cake pans. Line bottoms with wax paper; butter paper.

2   Combine bread crumbs, walnuts, and baking powder in a medium bowl. Beat egg whites with salt in a large bowl at medium speed to soft peaks. Gradually add sugar and continue beating until stiff. Whisk yolks in another bowl until light. Fold one-fourth of the beaten whites into the yolks with a rubber spatula. Fold in the crumb mixture, then the remaining whites just until blended.

3   Spread batter evenly in prepared pans. Bake 30 minutes or until golden and edges of cakes begin to shrink from sides of pans. Cool in pans on wire racks 10 minutes. With a small knife, loosen sides of cakes from pans. Invert onto wire racks, peel off wax paper and cool completely.

4   In a large mixing bowl beat cream with cinnamon and vanilla until stiff. Spoon ⅓ cup whipped cream into a pastry bag fitted with a star tip. Place a cake layer on a serving plate and spread with half the remaining whipped cream. Add second cake layer and spread with ⅔ cup jam. Top with third layer; spread with remaining cream. Pipe reserved whipped cream on top to form a 2-inch ring. Fill ring with 1 tablespoon jam. Refrigerate up to 4 hours before serving. Makes 12 servings.

PER SERVING		DAILY GOAL
Calories	375	2,000 (F), 2,500 (M)
Total Fat	24 g	60 g or less (F), 70 g or less (M)
Saturated fat	11 g	20 g or less (F), 23 g or less (M)
Cholesterol	163 mg	300 mg or less
Sodium	123 mg	2,400 mg or less
Carbohydrates	35g	250 g or more
Protein	6 g	55 g to 90 g

NOTES

_____

_____

_____

_____

_____

_____

_____

_____

CARROT CAKE WITH CREAM CHEESE ICING

This is without doubt our favorite American spice cake. It's best if you prepare the layers a day ahead to allow the flavors to develop.

Prep time: 30 minutes plus cooling
Baking time: 40 to 45 minutes
Degree of difficulty: easy

- 2 **cups all-purpose flour**
- 2 **teaspoons baking soda**
- 2 **teaspoons cinnamon**
- 1 **teaspoon salt**
- ½ **teaspoon nutmeg**
  Pinch cloves
- 4 **large eggs**
- 1 **cup granulated sugar**
- ¾ **cup packed brown sugar**
- 1 **teaspoon vanilla extract**
- 1 **cup vegetable oil**
- 3 **cups (about 1 pound) shredded carrots**
- ¾ **cup chopped walnuts**

Cream Cheese Icing

- 1 **package (8 ounces) cream cheese, softened**
- ¼ **cup butter *or* margarine**
- 1 **teaspoon vanilla extract**
- ½ **teaspoon grated orange peel**
- 3 **cups confectioners' sugar**
- ½ **cup finely chopped walnuts, for garnish**

1 Preheat oven to 350°F. Butter two 8-inch square or 9-inch round cake pans. Line bottoms with wax paper. Butter and flour paper; tap to remove excess flour.

2 Combine flour, baking soda, cinnamon, salt, nutmeg, and cloves in a small bowl. Combine eggs, granulated sugar, brown sugar, and vanilla in a large mixing bowl and beat at medium speed until smooth. With mixer at low speed, gradually add oil in a thin, steady stream until blended. Add dry ingredients and beat just until blended. Fold in carrots and nuts with a rubber spatula. Spoon into prepared pans.

3 Bake 40 to 45 minutes or until cake tester inserted in center comes out clean. Cool in pans on wire rack 10 minutes. Invert cakes onto racks. Carefully peel off wax paper, then cool completely, right side up. (Can be made ahead. Wrap well and store at room temperature up to 24 hours.)

4 Place a layer on cake plate and spread with one-third of icing. Top with second layer. Spread top and sides with remaining icing. Press nuts along sides of cake. Makes 16 servings.

Cream Cheese Icing: Combine cream cheese, butter, vanilla, and orange peel in a large mixing bowl. Beat at medium-high speed until light and fluffy, scraping bowl occasionally. Beat in confectioners' sugar to a spreading consistency.

PER SERVING		DAILY GOAL
Calories	530	2,000 (F), 2,500 (M)
Total Fat	29 g	60 g or less (F), 70 g or less (M)
Saturated fat	8 g	20 g or less (F), 23 g or less (M)
Cholesterol	76 mg	300 mg or less
Sodium	398 mg	2,400 mg or less
Carbohydrates	63 g	250 g or more
Protein	6 g	55 g to 90 g

CLASSIC GERMAN CHOCOLATE CAKE

Texas is the origin of this triple layer cake, named for Sam German, who developed the chocolate.

Prep time: 45 minutes plus cooling
Baking time: 30 to 35 minutes
Degree of difficulty: moderate

- 1 bar (4 ounces) sweet baking chocolate, cut up
- ½ cup boiling water
- ¾ cup sour cream
- ¼ cup milk
- 1 cup butter *or* margarine, softened
- 1¾ cups granulated sugar
- 4 large eggs, separated, at room temperature
- 1 teaspoon vanilla extract
- 2 cups all-purpose flour
- 1 teaspoon baking soda
- ½ teaspoon salt

Frosting
- 1 cup evaporated milk
- 1 cup granulated sugar
- 3 large egg yolks, lightly beaten
- ½ cup butter *or* margarine
- 1 teaspoon vanilla extract
- 2 cups shredded coconut
- 1½ cups pecans, chopped

1 Preheat oven to 350°F. Butter three 9-inch round cake pans. Line bottoms with wax paper. Butter and flour paper; tap to remove excess flour.

2 Stir chocolate and boiling water together in a small bowl until chocolate melts; cool. Stir sour cream and milk together in another small bowl. Beat butter and sugar in a large mixing bowl until light and fluffy. Add egg yolks 1 at a time, beating well after each addition. Gradually beat in melted chocolate and vanilla until smooth. With mixer at low speed, add dry ingredients alternating with sour cream mixture, beginning and ending with dry ingredients.

3 Beat egg whites in a clean mixing bowl at medium-high speed until stiff but not dry. Gently fold into chocolate batter with a rubber spatula. Pour into prepared pans. Bake 30 to 35 minutes, or until toothpick inserted in center comes out clean. Cool in pans on wire racks 10 minutes. Invert cakes onto racks. Carefully peel off wax paper then cool completely, right side up.

4 Place a layer on cake plate and spread with one-fourth of frosting. Top with second layer and spread with one-fourth of icing. Add third layer and spread top and sides with remaining icing. Makes 16 servings.

Frosting: Combine evaporated milk, sugar, egg yolks, butter, and vanilla in a large saucepan. Cook, stirring, over medium heat until thickened, about 12 minutes *(do not boil)*. Stir in coconut and pecans; cool, stirring occasionally.

PER SERVING		DAILY GOAL
Calories	580	2,000 (F), 2,500 (M)
Total Fat	36 g	60 g or less (F), 70 g or less (M)
Saturated fat	18 g	20 g or less (F), 23 g or less (M)
Cholesterol	150 mg	300 mg or less
Sodium	397 mg	2,400 mg or less
Carbohydrates	60 g	250 g or more
Protein	7 g	55 g to 90 g

NOTES

_____

_____

_____

_____

_____

_____

DESSERTS FOR

COMFORT

Sweet serenity is easy when you can snuggle up on a cold winter's day to a heaping helping of Warm Cranberry Cake with Orange Whipped Cream, Warm Banana Puff with Chocolate Sauce, or Apple-Pear Brown Betty with a cinnamon custard sauce. If that's not enough, company will come running when you offer the creamy comfort of our Tiramisu, Classic Crème Brûlée or Floating Islands in Caramel Cages. Simply divine!

BREAD AND BUTTER PUDDING

This old-fashioned English dessert features layers of bread spread with sweet butter and strawberry jam.

Prep time: 30 minutes plus standing
Baking time: 1 hour
○ *Degree of difficulty: easy*

¼ **cup currants**

¼ **cup golden raisins**

6 **tablespoons butter** *or* **margarine, softened**

18 **slices firm white bread, crusts removed**

6 **tablespoons strawberry jam**

5 **large eggs**

¼ **cup granulated sugar**

1 **teaspoon vanilla extract**

¼ **teaspoon cinnamon**

¼ **teaspoon nutmeg**

¼ **teaspoon salt**

3 **cups milk**

1 **cup heavy** *or* **whipping cream**

1 Butter a 12x7½x2-inch baking dish. Combine currants and raisins in a small bowl; set aside.

2 Spread softened butter on one side of each bread slice. Place bread, buttered side down, on a large sheet of wax paper and spread strawberry jam over tops. Place 6 bread slices, buttered side down, in prepared baking dish. Sprinkle with half the currants and raisins. Repeat layering another 6 bread slices and remaining currants and raisins. Top with remaining 6 bread slices, jam side up.

3 Preheat oven to 350°F. Whisk together eggs, sugar, vanilla, cinnamon, nutmeg, and salt in a large bowl. Whisk in milk and cream until well combined; pour evenly over bread. Let stand at room temperature 30 minutes.

4 Bake pudding 1 hour or until top is puffed and golden brown and a knife inserted in center comes out clean. Let stand 10 minutes before serving. Makes 12 servings.

PER SERVING		DAILY GOAL
Calories	355	2,000 (F), 2,500 (M)
Total Fat	19 g	60 g or less (F), 70 g or less (M)
Saturated fat	11 g	20 g or less (F), 23 g or less (M)
Cholesterol	141 mg	300 mg or less
Sodium	381 mg	2,400 mg or less
Carbohydrates	38 g	250 g or more
Protein	9 g	55 g to 90 g

NOTES

FIGGY PUDDING

Steamed pudding is our favorite yuletide tradition. You don't need a pudding mold—any heat-proof bowl can be used. We prefer to make it ahead of time to let the flavors blend.

Prep time: 20 minutes plus standing
Cooking time: 2½ hours
○ *Degree of difficulty: easy*

2   **large eggs, beaten**
1   **cup granulated sugar**
1   **cup shredded, peeled Granny Smith apple**
1   **package (8 ounces) Calimyrna figs, chopped fine**
½   **cup raisins**
½   **cup butter *or* margarine, melted**
3   **tablespoons brandy**
1   **cup all-purpose flour**
2   **teaspoons baking powder**
1   **teaspoon cinnamon**
½   **teaspoon ginger**
¼   **teaspoon salt**
     Sweetened whipped cream

1 Grease a 1½-quart steamed pudding mold or heat-proof bowl. Combine eggs, sugar, apple, figs, raisins, butter, and brandy in a large bowl. Combine flour, baking powder, cinnamon, ginger, and salt in a medium bowl stir into fig mixture. Pour into prepared mold and cover tightly with a lid or foil.

2 Place mold on a wire rack in a large Dutch oven. Pour boiling water halfway up outside of mold. Cover and simmer over medium-low heat 2½ hours. Remove from water bath and let stand 15 minutes. Carefully unmold onto a wire rack to cool. Wrap in foil and let stand at room temperature overnight. (Can be made ahead. Refrigerate up to 2 weeks. To reheat, return pudding to mold and steam 1 hour or heat, wrapped in foil, in a preheated 350°F. oven 1 hour.) Unwrap and serve pudding warm with sweetened whipped cream. Makes 12 servings.

PER 1/2 CUP SERVING		DAILY GOAL
Calories	265	2,000 (F), 2,500 (M)
Total Fat	9 g	60 g or less (F), 70 g or less (M)
Saturated fat	5 g	20 g or less (F), 23 g or less (M)
Cholesterol	56 mg	300 mg or less
Sodium	208 mg	2,400 mg or less
Carbohydrates	43 g	250 g or more
Protein	3 g	55 g to 90 g

APPLE-PEAR BROWN BETTY

This baked pudding of spiced fruit and buttery bread crumbs is pure heaven served warm with a velvety cinnamon custard sauce. *Also pictured on page 110.*

Prep time: 25 minutes
Baking time: 1 hour
○ *Degree of difficulty: easy*

3 **Granny Smith apples, peeled and thinly sliced**
3 **ripe pears, peeled and thinly sliced**
1 **tablespoon fresh lemon juice**
5 **slices white *or* whole wheat bread, cubed**
¼ **cup butter *or* margarine, melted**
1 **tablespoon granulated sugar**
⅔ **cup firmly packed brown sugar**
½ **teaspoon grated lemon peel**
¼ **teaspoon cinnamon**
⅛ **teaspoon nutmeg**
 Cinnamon-Vanilla Custard Sauce (recipe at right)

1 Preheat oven to 375°F. Butter a 9-inch square baking dish. Toss apples and pears with lemon juice in a large bowl. Toss bread cubes with butter and granulated sugar in a medium bowl. Combine brown sugar, lemon peel, cinnamon, and nutmeg in another bowl.

2 Spread half the fruit mixture in the prepared baking dish. Sprinkle with half the bread cubes then half the brown sugar mixture; repeat layering. Cover and bake 30 minutes. Uncover and bake 30 minutes more or until top is golden and fruit is bubbly. Serve with Cinnamon-Vanilla Custard Sauce. Makes 6 servings.

PER SERVING WITHOUT SAUCE		DAILY GOAL
Calories	405	2,000 (F), 2,500 (M)
Total Fat	13 g	60 g or less (F), 70 g or less (M)
Saturated fat	7 g	20 g or less (F), 23 g or less (M)
Cholesterol	134 mg	300 mg or less
Sodium	228 mg	2,400 mg or less
Carbohydrates	70 g	250 g or more
Protein	5 g	55 g to 90 g

CINNAMON-VANILLA CUSTARD SAUCE

Prep time: 10 minutes plus chilling
◑ *Degree of difficulty: moderate*

1 **vanilla bean or 1 teaspoon vanilla extract**
1¼ **cups milk**
1 **cinnamon stick**
3 **large egg yolks**
¼ **cup sugar**

1 Split vanilla bean in half lengthwise and scrap out seeds. Place bean and seeds in small saucepan with milk and cinnamon stick and bring to boil.

2 Meanwhile, whisk egg yolks and sugar together in a small bowl. Gradually whisk in hot milk. Return to saucepan and cook, stirring constantly, over medium heat until mixture thickens slightly and coats the back of a spoon, about 5 minutes *(do not boil).* Strain through a fine sieve into a medium bowl, discarding vanilla bean and cinnamon stick. Refrigerate until cold, 2 hours. Makes 1⅓ cups.

PER TABLESPOON		DAILY GOAL
Calories	27	2,000 (F), 2,500 (M)
Total Fat	1 g	60 g or less (F), 70 g or less (M)
Saturated fat	1 g	20 g or less (F), 23 g or less (M)
Cholesterol	32 mg	300 mg or less
Sodium	8 mg	2,400 mg or less
Carbohydrates	3 g	250 g or more
Protein	1 g	55 g to 90 g

CLASSIC CRÈME BRÛLÉE

This silky, elegant custard with a crackling caramel topping is the ultimate in French desserts.

Prep time: 20 minutes plus standing and chilling
Baking time: 25 to 30 minutes
Degree of difficulty: moderate

2 **cups heavy** *or* **whipping cream**
1 **cup half-and-half cream**
1 **vanilla bean** *or* **1 tablespoon vanilla extract**
6 **large egg yolks**
¾ **cup granulated sugar, divided**
   Assorted sliced fruit, optional

1 Preheat oven to 300°F. Combine heavy cream and half-and-half cream in a medium saucepan. Bring just to a boil over medium heat. Split vanilla bean lengthwise and scrape out seeds. Add bean and seeds to hot cream mixture. Cover and let stand 15 minutes.

2 Combine egg yolks and ½ cup of the sugar in a medium bowl and whisk until light. Gradually whisk in ½ cup warm cream. Whisking constantly, pour in remaining cream; continue whisking until smooth. (Stir in vanilla extract, if using.)

3 Strain custard through a fine sieve into a shallow 1-quart baking or gratin dish. Discard vanilla bean. Skim any foam off top of custard. Place dish in a large roasting pan. Carefully pour enough boiling water into roasting pan to come halfway up side of dish. Bake 25 to 30 minutes, until custard is barely set in center. (*Do not overbake.* Custard will set as it cools.) Let stand in water bath 10 minutes. Carefully transfer to a wire rack and cool completely. Cover and refrigerate 3 hours or overnight.

4 Preheat broiler. Sprinkle top of custard with the remaining ¼ cup sugar. Place dish in a roasting pan. Carefully pour ice water into roasting pan to come halfway up side of dish. Broil 3 inches from heat, rotating pan if necessary, 2 to 3 minutes or until sugar is melted and a dark amber color. Cool custard in ice water 5 minutes. Remove from roasting pan and refrigerate 15 to 20 minutes before serving. Serve with sliced fruit.

PER SERVING WITHOUT FRUIT		DAILY GOAL
Calories	365	2,000 (F), 2,500 (M)
Total Fat	29 g	60 g or less (F), 70 g or less (M)
Saturated fat	17 g	20 g or less (F), 23 g or less (M)
Cholesterol	252 mg	300 mg or less
Sodium	40 mg	2,400 mg or less
Carbohydrates	22 g	250 g or more
Protein	4 g	55 g to 90 g

NOTES

PUMPKIN CRÈME CARAMEL

Here's a velvety custard with just the right touch of pumpkin and fresh ginger and made complete with a soothing caramel syrup.

Prep time: 35 minutes
Baking time: 1 hour
○ *Degree of difficulty: moderate*

1 **cup granulated sugar, divided**
⅓ **cup water**
1 **cup milk**
1 **cup heavy *or* whipping cream**
¼ **teaspoon salt**
1 **2-ounce piece (⅓ cup) ginger, peeled and cut into ¼-inch slices**
5 **large eggs**
1 **large egg yolk**
1 **teaspoon vanilla extract**
1 **cup solid pack pumpkin**

1 Dissolve ⅔ cup of the sugar and the water in a medium saucepan over medium-high heat. Bring to a boil. Boil, stirring occasionally, until syrup is a golden brown, about 8 to 10 minutes. Meanwhile, warm a 1½-quart soufflé dish in hot tap water. Remove dish from water and immediately pour in caramel syrup, tilting dish to coat bottom evenly. Set aside and keep warm.

2 Preheat oven to 350°F. Combine milk, cream, the remaining ⅓ cup sugar, salt, and ginger in a medium saucepan. Bring to a boil; remove from heat. Meanwhile, whisk together eggs, egg yolks, and vanilla in a large bowl. Beating constantly, gradually add hot milk mixture to egg mixture, then strain through a fine sieve into another large bowl; discard ginger. Whisk pumpkin into custard until smooth. Pour into prepared soufflé dish.

3 Place dish in a large roasting pan. Carefully pour enough boiling water into roasting pan to reach halfway up side of dish. Place in oven and immediately reduce temperature to 325°F. Bake 1 hour or until a knife inserted in center comes out clean. Remove from water bath and transfer to a wire rack. Cool completely. Cover and refrigerate 4 hours or overnight. To serve, run a knife around edge of custard and invert onto a large serving plate. Makes 10 servings.

PER SERVING		DAILY GOAL
Calories	210	2,000 (F), 2,500 (M)
Total Fat	12 g	60 g or less (F), 70 g or less (M)
Saturated fat	6 g	20 g or less (F), 23 g or less (M)
Cholesterol	149 mg	300 mg or less
Sodium	99 mg	2,400 mg or less
Carbohydrates	23 g	250 g or more
Protein	5 g	55 g to 90 g

NOTES

_____
_____
_____
_____
_____
_____
_____
_____
_____
_____
_____
_____
_____
_____

CAPPUCCINO SOUFFLÉ

A dessert soufflé is always a show-stopper. Espresso and a touch of cinnamon make this version extra special.

Prep time: 30 minutes
Baking time: 35 to 40 minutes
Degree of difficulty: moderate

½ cup plus 2 tablespoons granulated sugar, divided
½ cup all-purpose flour
⅛ teaspoon cinnamon
¾ cup milk, divided
4 large egg yolks
¼ cup brewed espresso *or* 2 tablespoons instant espresso powder dissolved in ¼ cup boiling water
2 teaspoons vanilla extract
5 large egg whites, at room temperature
⅛ teaspoon cream of tartar
Confectioners' sugar and grated semisweet chocolate, for garnish

Chocolate Sauce
4 squares (4 ounces) unsweetened chocolate, coarsely chopped
1 cup heavy *or* whipping cream
6 tablespoons granulated sugar

Cognac Whipped Cream
1 cup heavy *or* whipping cream
2 tablespoons granulated sugar
1 tablespoon cognac

1 Preheat oven to 400°F. Butter a 6-cup soufflé dish and coat bottom and sides with 1 tablespoon of the sugar.

2 Combine flour, ½ cup of the sugar, and the cinnamon in a large saucepan. Add ¼ cup of the milk and whisk until smooth. Gradually whisk in remaining ½ cup milk; continue whisking until smooth. Cook over medium heat, stirring constantly, until very thick and smooth; cook 30 seconds more. Remove from heat and beat in egg yolks 1 at a time. Beat in espresso and vanilla. Transfer to a large bowl; cover surface with plastic wrap and cool.

3 Beat egg whites in a large mixing bowl on medium speed until frothy. Add cream of tartar and continue to beat to soft peaks. Add the remaining 1 tablespoon sugar and

beat until peaks are stiff but not dry. Add one-fourth of the whites to the egg yolk base and gently fold with a rubber spatula until blended. Fold in remaining whites. Gently pour into prepared dish.

4 Place dish in oven and immediately reduce heat to 375°F. Bake 35 to 40 minutes or until puffed and top is lightly browned. Sprinkle top of soufflé with sifted confectioners' sugar, then grated chocolate. Serve immediately with warm Chocolate Sauce and Cognac Whipped Cream. Makes 6 servings.

Chocolate Sauce: Combine chocolate, cream, and sugar in a small saucepan. Heat over medium-low heat, whisking constantly, until smooth.

Cognac Whipped Cream: Whip cream, sugar, and cognac in a large mixing bowl to soft peaks.

PER SERVING		DAILY GOAL	
Calories	480	2,000 (F), 2,500 (M)	
Total Fat	29 g	60 g or less (F), 70 g or less (M)	
Saturated fat	17 g	20 g or less (F), 23 g or less (M)	
Cholesterol	200 mg	300 mg or less	
Sodium	83 mg	2,400 mg or less	
Carbohydrates	50 g	250 g or more	
Protein	9 g	55 g to 90 g	

OUR BEST RICE PUDDING

Cooking the rice very slowly in the milk is the key to this homey pudding dessert.

Prep time: 10 minutes plus chilling
Cooking time: 1 hour
○ *Degree of difficulty: easy*

1 **quart milk**
½ **vanilla bean, split,** *or* **2 teaspoons vanilla extract**
½ **cup long-grain rice, uncooked**
⅓ **cup granulated sugar**
2 **large egg yolks**
¼ **teaspoon salt**
⅔ **cup heavy** *or* **whipping cream**

1 Heat milk with vanilla bean to boiling in a medium saucepan over medium-high heat. Stir in rice and return to a boil. Reduce heat and simmer uncovered, stirring occasionally, until rice is tender, about 55 minutes.

2 Meanwhile, whisk together sugar, egg yolks, and salt in a medium bowl until blended. Pour in cream and whisk again until completely blended and smooth.

3 When rice is done, remove from heat and stir in cream mixture until well combined. Return to a boil over medium-high heat; remove and discard vanilla bean. (Stir in vanilla extract, if using.)

4 Pour pudding into a 6-cup serving dish. Cool to room temperature. Cover and refrigerate 4 hours or overnight. Makes 8 servings.

PER SERVING		DAILY GOAL
Calories	315	2,000 (F), 2,500 (M)
Total Fat	17 g	60 g or less (F), 70 g or less (M)
Saturated fat	10 g	20 g or less (F), 23 g or less (M)
Cholesterol	130 mg	300 mg or less
Sodium	183 mg	2,400 mg or less
Carbohydrates	32 g	250 g or more
Protein	8 g	55 g to 90 g

A TOAST TO NUTS

For any recipe, toasting nuts heightens their flavor. Here's how:

Oven: Preheat oven to 350°F. Spread nuts on a baking sheet in a single layer. Bake 8 to 10 minutes until lightly toasted and fragrant, stirring once. Cool completely.

Microwave: Cover bottom of your microwave oven with wax paper. Spread with ½ cup chopped nuts. Microwave uncovered on high (100% power) 3 to 5 minutes or until lightly browned, stirring once.

FLOATING ISLANDS IN CARAMEL CAGES

The custard for this breathtaking dessert can be prepared ahead, but the meringues and caramel should be served the day they're made.

Prep time: 1 hour plus chilling
Baking time: 16 minutes
Degree of difficulty: moderate

1 **cup milk**
½ **cup heavy** *or* **whipping cream**
4 **large egg yolks**
⅓ **cup granulated sugar**
3 **teaspoons vanilla extract, divided**
½ **cup plus 3 tablespoons sugar**
4 **large egg whites, at room temperature**
   Pinch cream of tartar

Caramel Cages
1 **cup granulated sugar**
2 **tablespoons water**

1 For custard, heat milk and cream to boiling in a medium saucepan. Meanwhile, whisk egg yolks and sugar together in a small bowl. Gradually whisk in hot milk. Return to saucepan and cook, stirring constantly, over medium heat, until mixture thickens slightly and coats the back of a spoon, about 5 minutes *(do not boil)*. Strain through a fine sieve into a medium bowl; stir in 2 teaspoons of the vanilla. Cover and refrigerate until cold, 2 hours.

2 Preheat oven to 325°F. For meringues, grease 6 Bundtlette pan cups* or 6-ounce Pyrex custard cups and sprinkle with 3 tablespoons sugar. Beat egg whites in a large mixing bowl until frothy. Add cream of tartar and continue beating to soft peaks. Gradually beat in the remaining ½ cup sugar. Add the remaining 1 teaspoon vanilla; beat at high speed until stiff and glossy, about 1 minute more.

3 Pack meringue evenly into Bundtlette cups. Place in a roasting pan. Place in oven and carefully pour enough boiling water into roasting pan to come 1 inch up sides of pans. Bake 16 minutes or until toothpick inserted in center of one meringue comes out clean. Remove pan from water and cool. (Meringues will fall as they cool.) Invert meringues onto dessert plates.

4 To assemble, spoon custard around meringue and top each with a Caramel Cage. Pass additional custard. Makes 6 servings.

Caramel Cages: Combine sugar and water in a medium saucepan. Cook over medium-high heat, stirring with a wooden spoon just until sugar dissolves. Then bring to a boil without stirring. Cook to a deep amber color. Remove pan from heat and carefully place in a bowl of cool water for 30 seconds. Spray the outside of an inverted Bundtlette pan with vegetable cooking spray. (Or brush outside of six 6-ounce custard cups with vegetable oil.) Carefully drizzle hot caramel over each mold. (If caramel is too thick to drizzle, reheat over medium heat.) Cool 15 minutes. Carefully loosen caramel and lift off cages.

*Bundtlette pans can be ordered from Nordic Ware (800-328-4310)

PER SERVING WITH 3 TABLESPOONS CUSTARD		DAILY GOAL
Calories	410	2,000 (F), 2,500 (M)
Total Fat	12 g	60 g or less (F), 70 g or less (M)
Saturated fat	6 g	20 g or less (F), 23 g or less (M)
Cholesterol	175 mg	300 mg or less
Sodium	69 mg	2,400 mg or less
Carbohydrates	71 g	250 g or more
Protein	6 g	55 g to 90 g

PINEAPPLE FOSTER

Our spectacular version of the famed New Orleans dessert, Bananas Foster, is made easier if you buy the pineapple already peeled and cored.

Prep time: 10 minutes
Cooking time: 6 minutes
⬤ *Degree of difficulty: easy*

1   **ripe pineapple, peeled, cored, and cut into 12 spears**
¾   **cup firmly packed brown sugar**
½   **cup dark rum**
¼   **cup hazelnut liqueur**
2   **tablespoons butter
    (no substitutions)**
1   **pint premium vanilla ice cream**
⅓   **cup macadamia nuts *or* pecans**

1 Heat a large cast-iron skillet over high heat until smoking. Meanwhile, toss pineapple with brown sugar in a large bowl until well coated. Add pineapple in a single layer to skillet, in batches if necessary. Cook until glazed on both sides, about 30 seconds per side. Remove from pan and set aside.

2 Add rum, liqueur, butter, and any sugar remaining in bowl to skillet. (If mixture ignites, cover skillet with a lid to extinguish.) Bring to a boil. Cook, stirring, until mixture is syrupy, 3 minutes.

3 To serve, place a scoop of ice cream on each of 6 dessert plates. Spoon on pineapple and sauce. Sprinkle with nuts. Makes 6 servings.

PER SERVING		DAILY GOAL
Calories	420	2,000 (F), 2,500 (M)
Total Fat	18 g	60 g or less (F), 70 g or less (M)
Saturated fat	8 g	20 g or less (F), 23 g or less (M)
Cholesterol	39 mg	300 mg or less
Sodium	85 mg	2,400 mg or less
Carbohydrates	52 g	250 g or more
Protein	2 g	55 g to 90 g

TOASTING AND SKINNING HAZELNUTS

Preheat oven to 350°F. Spread hazelnuts on a baking sheet in a single layer. Bake until lightly browned and skins are crackly, 12 to 15 minutes. Wrap nuts in a clean kitchen towel and let stand 5 minutes. Rub nuts in towel to remove skins, then cool completely.

NOTES

WARM BANANA PUFF WITH CHOCOLATE SAUCE

Here's the perfect way to use those ripe, brown bananas. Serve with ice cream, and you got all the flavors of a banana split!

Prep time: 20 minutes
Baking time: 35 minutes
Degree of difficulty: moderate

1 **cup mashed ripe bananas**
1 **tablespoon fresh lemon juice**
3 **tablespoons butter** *or* **margarine**
⅓ **cup all-purpose flour**
¾ **cup milk, heated to boiling**
4 **large eggs, at room temperature, separated**
½ **cup plus 2 tablespoons granulated sugar, divided**
¼ **teaspoon cinnamon**
⅛ **teaspoon nutmeg**

Chocolate Sauce
½ **cup heavy** *or* **whipping cream**
3 **squares (3 ounces) semisweet chocolate**
2 **ripe bananas, sliced**

1 Preheat oven to 375°F. Grease a shallow 2-quart baking dish; sprinkle with 2 tablespoons of the sugar. Combine bananas with lemon juice; set aside.

2 Melt butter in a medium saucepan over medium heat. Add flour and cook, whisking, 1 minute. Pour in hot milk and cook, whisking, until thickened. Remove from heat and whisk in banana mixture, then egg yolks, cinnamon, and nutmeg.

3 Beat egg whites in a large mixing bowl until foamy. Beat in the remaining ½ cup sugar and continue to beat until stiff and glossy. Fold half the beaten whites into the banana mixture with a rubber spatula, then gently fold in remaining whites. Pour into prepared baking dish and bake 30 minutes or until almost firm in center. Serve immediately with Chocolate Sauce and sliced bananas. Makes 6 servings.

Chocolate Sauce: Combine cream and chocolate in small microwave-proof bowl. Microwave on high (100% power) 3 minutes, stirring every minute until smooth. Makes ⅔ cup.

PER SERVING WITH
CHOCOLATE SAUCE

		DAILY GOAL
Calories	435	2,000 (F), 2,500 (M)
Total Fat	23 g	60 g or less (F), 70 g or less (M)
Saturated fat	13 g	20 g or less (F), 23 g or less (M)
Cholesterol	190 mg	300 mg or less
Sodium	132 mg	2,400 mg or less
Carbohydrates	55 g	250 g or more
Protein	8 g	55 g to 90 g

NOTES

123

TIRAMISU

There are many variations of this classic dessert, but only the real thing contains espresso and mascarpone cheese.

Prep time: 35 minutes plus chilling
Baking time: 12 to 15 minutes
Degree of difficulty: moderate

4   **large eggs, at room temperature**
1   **cup plus 2 tablespoons granulated sugar, divided**
1   **teaspoon vanilla extract**
¾   **cup all-purpose flour**
¼   **teaspoon salt**
½   **cup brewed espresso coffee**
¼   **cup brandy**
1   **pound mascarpone cheese**
1   **cup heavy *or* whipping cream**
2   **teaspoons unsweetened cocoa**
½   **cup heavy *or* whipping cream, whipped**

1 For sponge cake, preheat oven to 350°F. Grease a 15½x10½-inch jelly-roll pan. Line with wax paper; grease and flour paper and tap out excess flour.

2 Beat eggs and ¾ cup of the sugar in a large mixing bowl at high speed until mixture forms a ribbon when beaters are lifted, about 10 minutes. Beat in vanilla. Combine flour and salt in a small bowl. Sift onto egg mixture, then gently fold in with a rubber spatula. Spread into prepared pan. Bake 12 to 15 minutes or until top springs back when lightly touched. Cool in pan on wire rack.

3 For syrup, combine coffee, brandy, and 2 tablespoons of the sugar, stirring, until sugar is dissolved.

4 For filling, blend mascarpone with the remaining ¼ cup sugar in a large bowl. Beat the 1 cup cream in a clean mixing bowl with clean beaters to stiff peaks; fold into mascarpone mixture with a rubber spatula.

5 To assemble, unmold cake and peel off paper. Cut cake in half. Trim each half to fit a shallow 2-quart glass or ceramic dish. Place a layer on bottom of dish. Drizzle evenly with half the syrup; spoon on half the filling. Place remaining cake layer on top, drizzle with remaining syrup and spread top with remaining filling. Sift cocoa over filling. Cover and refrigerate overnight. Pipe the whipped cream decoratively on top. Makes 12 servings.

PER SERVING		DAILY GOAL	
Calories	415	2,000 (F), 2,500 (M)	
Total Fat	30 g	60 g or less (F), 70 g or less (M)	
Saturated fat	7 g	20 g or less (F), 23 g or less (M)	
Cholesterol	164 mg	300 mg or less	
Sodium	101 mg	2,400 mg or less	
Carbohydrates	28 g	250 g or more	
Protein	6 g	55 g to 90 g	

NOTES

_____

_____

_____

_____

_____

_____

_____

_____

_____

_____

_____

_____

_____

_____

_____

WARM CRANBERRY CAKE WITH ORANGE WHIPPED CREAM

This comfy cake can also be enjoyed in the summer months: Substitute blueberries for the cranberries, and lemon peel for the orange peel and serve with vanilla ice cream.

Prep time: 25 minutes
Baking time: 45 minutes
○ *Degree of difficulty: easy*

- 2 **cups all-purpose flour**
- 2 **teaspoons baking powder**
- ½ **teaspoon salt**
- ½ **cup butter *or* margarine, softened**
- 1 **cup plus 2 tablespoons granulated sugar, divided**
- 2 **large eggs**
- 1 **tablespoon fresh orange juice**
- 1 **teaspoon grated orange peel**
- ½ **cup milk**
- 1 **cup fresh cranberries, divided**

Orange Whipped Cream
- 1 **cup heavy *or* whipping cream**
- 2 **tablespoons granulated sugar**
- 2 **tablespoons orange-flavored liqueur**

1 Preheat oven to 375°F. Butter a 9-inch springform pan. Line bottom with wax paper; butter and flour paper and tap to remove excess flour.

2 Combine flour, baking powder, and salt in a medium bowl. Beat butter and 1 cup of the sugar in a large mixing bowl at medium-high speed until light and fluffy. Add eggs, 1 at a time, beating well after each addition. Add orange juice and orange peel. At low speed, gradually beat in dry ingredients alternating with milk, beginning and ending with dry ingredients.

3 Chop ½ cup of the cranberries and stir into batter. Pour batter into prepared pan. Sprinkle top with the remaining cranberries and the remaining 2 tablespoons sugar.

4 Bake 40 minutes or until toothpick inserted in center comes out clean. Cool in pan on a wire rack 10 minutes. Remove sides of pan. Serve warm with Orange Whipped Cream. Makes 10 servings.

Orange Whipped Cream: Beat cream and sugar in a large, chilled mixing bowl with chilled beaters until stiff. Beat in liqueur.

PER SERVING		DAILY GOAL
Calories	390	2,000 (F), 2,500 (M)
Total Fat	20 g	60 g or less (F), 70 g or less (M)
Saturated fat	12 g	20 g or less (F), 23 g or less (M)
Cholesterol	103 mg	300 mg or less
Sodium	333 mg	2,400 mg or less
Carbohydrates	48 g	250 g or more
Protein	5 g	55 g to 90 g

NOTES

FRESH GINGER CAKE WITH SAUTÉED APPLES

All dressed up with apples and whipped cream, this American favorite gets its great flavor from freshly grated ginger.

Prep time: 30 minutes
Baking time: 30 minutes
O *Degree of difficulty: easy*

1 **cup unsulfured molasses**
½ **cup buttermilk**
¼ **cup butter** *or* **margarine, melted**
1 **large egg**
1 **tablespoon freshly grated ginger**
2 **cups all-purpose flour**
1 **teaspoon baking soda**
½ **teaspoon salt**

Sautéed Apples
3 **tablespoons butter** *or* **margarine**
3 **tablespoons firmly packed brown sugar**
2 **tablespoons dark rum**
4 **Rome apples, peeled and sliced**

Whipped Cream
1 **cup heavy** *or* **whipping cream**
2 **tablespoons packed brown sugar**
½ **teaspoon vanilla extract**

1 Preheat oven to 375°F. Butter a 9-inch square baking pan. Whisk together molasses, buttermilk, butter, egg, and ginger in a large bowl until smooth. Add flour, baking soda, and salt; whisk until smooth. Pour into prepared pan.

2 Bake 30 minutes or until toothpick inserted in center comes out clean. Cool in pan on a wire rack. Cut into squares and serve with Sautéed Apples and Whipped Cream. Makes 9 servings.

Sautéed Apples: Melt butter in a large skillet over medium-high heat. Stir in brown sugar and rum. Add apples and cook, stirring occasionally, until tender, 8 minutes.

Whipped Cream: Beat cream, brown sugar, and vanilla in a large mixing bowl until stiff.

PER SERVING		DAILY GOAL
Calories	460	2,000 (F), 2,500 (M)
Total Fat	20 g	60 g or less (F), 70 g or less (M)
Saturated fat	12 g	20 g or less (F), 23 g or less (M)
Cholesterol	85 mg	300 mg or less
Sodium	401 mg	2,400 mg or less
Carbohydrates	65 g	250 g or more
Protein	5 g	55 g to 90 g

NOTES

_____
_____
_____
_____
_____
_____
_____
_____
_____
_____
_____
_____
_____

SWEET AND

FRUITFUL

ENDINGS

Bursting with fresh fruit flavor, these light and luscious desserts will become seasonal favorites! Come celebrate the rites of spring with fresh Strawberries with Balsamic Vinegar. The fruits of July and August are simply splendid in our spectacular Classic Summer Pudding and giant Peaches 'n' Cream Shortcake. Or take away the first signs of winter's chill with warm Roasted Pears with Anisette. They're all a snap to make and each one presents fruit at its finest!

INDIVIDUAL PEAR SOUFFLÉS

We use pears packed in heavy syrup to give this dessert maximum fruit flavor. Brushing the individual baking dishes lightly with butter lends richness without much fat.

Ⓜ *Microwave*
Prep time: 30 minutes plus cooling
Baking time: 12 to 15 minutes
◑ *Degree of difficulty: moderate*

1 **tablespoon butter *or* margarine**
6 **tablespoons granulated sugar, divided**
3 **cans (16 ounces each) pears in heavy syrup, drained**
3 **tablespoons pear schnapps *or* pear brandy**
6 **large egg whites, at room temperature**
¼ **teaspoon cream of tartar**
 Pinch salt

1 In a microwave-proof 4-ounce ramekin or custard cup, microwave butter on high (100% power) 40 seconds. With a pastry brush, lightly spread butter on sides of ramekin, plus 7 more ramekins. Let stand until butter is cooled. Shake 2 tablespoons of the sugar around all ramekins to coat evenly.

2 Meanwhile, dice ½ cup pears; set aside. Puree remaining pears in a food processor until smooth. Transfer pureed pears to a large skillet and cook, stirring over high heat, until mixture is thickened and reduced to about 1 cup, 20 minutes. Transfer to a large bowl and stir in pear schnapps. Cool.

3 Preheat oven to 425°F. Beat egg whites with cream of tartar and salt in a large mixing bowl at medium speed until foamy. Increase speed to high. Gradually beat in the remaining 4 tablespoons sugar and continue to beat to stiff peaks. Gently stir one-third of the beaten whites into the pear mixture. Gently fold in remaining whites with a rubber spatula.

4 Spoon half the mixture into prepared ramekins. Sprinkle with diced pear and spoon remaining mixture on top. Place ramekins on a baking sheet. Bake 12 to 15 minutes or until tops are brown and firm. Serve immediately. Makes 8 servings.

PER SERVING		DAILY GOAL
Calories	205	2,000 (F), 2,500 (M)
Total Fat	2 g	60 g or less (F), 70 g or less (M)
Saturated fat	1 g	20 g or less (F), 23 g or less (M)
Cholesterol	4 mg	300 mg or less
Sodium	81 mg	2,400 mg or less
Carbohydrates	44 g	250 g or more
Protein	3 g	55 g to 90 g

NOTES

ROASTED PEARS WITH ANISETTE

Roasting brings out the richest flavor in pears, without the added fat. For this very refreshing dessert, the firmer Bosc variety pear works best.

Prep time: 10 minutes
Baking time: 50 minutes
○ *Degree of difficulty: easy*

2 **tablespoons butter *or* margarine, melted, divided**
10 **large ripe Bosc pears**
¼ **cup plus 5 teaspoons anisette *or* Sambuca liqueur, divided**
⅓ **cup granulated sugar**
½ **cup water**
1 **tablespoon fresh lemon juice**
1 **strip (3 inches) lemon peel**

1 Preheat oven to 425°F. Brush a shallow 2-quart baking dish with 1 teaspoon of the melted butter. With a small knife or apple corer, remove core of each pear, starting at the bottom and leaving the stem end intact. Brush ½ teaspoon of the liqueur into each pear cavity. Turn upright and transfer to prepared dish.

2 Brush pears with remaining melted butter and sprinkle sugar over tops. Add water, lemon juice, and lemon peel to the bottom of dish. Bake 40 minutes. Add the remaining ¼ cup liqueur and bake 10 minutes more or until pears are tender when pierced. Cool slightly. Serve warm with cooking juices. Makes 10 servings.

PER SERVING		DAILY GOAL
Calories	210	2,000 (F), 2,500 (M)
Total Fat	3 g	60 g or less (F), 70 g or less (M)
Saturated fat	1 g	20 g or less (F), 23 g or less (M)
Cholesterol	6 mg	300 mg or less
Sodium	23 mg	2,400 mg or less
Carbohydrates	43 g	250 g or more
Protein	1 g	55 g to 90 g

STRAWBERRIES WITH BALSAMIC VINEGAR

The Italians have always loved the pairing of fruit and mellow balsamic vinegar. Both low in fat and calories, this recipe can easily be doubled.

▼ *Low-fat*
▽ *Low-calorie*
  Prep time: 10 minutes plus standing
○ *Degree of difficulty: easy*

1 **pint strawberries, hulled and halved**
1 **tablespoon granulated sugar**
1½ **teaspoons balsamic vinegar**

Toss strawberries, sugar, and vinegar in a large bowl. Let stand 20 minutes, stirring occasionally. Makes 2 servings.

PER SERVING		DAILY GOAL
Calories	75	2,000 (F), 2,500 (M)
Total Fat	1 g	60 g or less (F), 70 g or less (M)
Saturated fat	0 g	20 g or less (F), 23 g or less (M)
Cholesterol	0 mg	300 mg or less
Sodium	2 mg	2,400 mg or less
Carbohydrates 1	8 g	250 g or more
Protein	1 g	55 g to 90 g

PEACHES 'N' CREAM SHORTCAKE

There's no better way to celebrate the harvest of peaches and nectarines than by making a shortcake. The subtle flavor and color of this pastry comes from a surprise ingredient—ground pecans. *Also pictured on page 128.*

Prep time: 50 minutes
Baking time: 24 to 25 minutes
Degree of difficulty: easy

- 2¼ **cups all-purpose flour**
- ½ **cup pecans, ground fine**
- 2 **teaspoons baking powder**
- ½ **teaspoon salt**
- 7 **tablespoons unsalted butter, softened (no substitutions)**
- 4 **tablespoons granulated sugar, divided**
- 2 **cups heavy *or* whipping cream, divided**
- 2 **tablespoons sour cream**
- ¼ **cup confectioners' sugar**
- 1 **teaspoon vanilla extract**
- 4 **cups thinly sliced peaches *or* nectarines, divided**
  Confectioners' sugar and mint sprigs, for garnish

1 For shortcake, preheat oven to 375°F. Line 2 cookie sheets with foil. Combine flour, ground nuts, baking powder, and salt in a medium bowl. Beat butter and 3 tablespoons of the granulated sugar in a larger mixing bowl until creamy. Add dry ingredients and beat at medium speed until mixture resembles fine crumbs.

2 Reserve 1 tablespoon cream. On low speed, add 1 cup of the cream to the pastry and beat just until blended. Turn pastry out onto a work surface and knead gently 3 or 4 times to form a smooth ball. Divide pastry into thirds.

3 On a lightly floured surface, roll each portion into an 8-inch circle. Carefully transfer circles to prepared cookie sheets. Brush evenly with reserved cream and sprinkle with remaining 1 tablespoon granulated sugar. With a long thin knife, score one circle into 8 wedges (*do not separate*). Bake 24 to 25 minutes, rotating cookie sheets once, until golden. Cool on foil from cookie sheets on wire racks. Remove foil and cut scored pastry into the 8 wedges. Set aside.

4 For filling, combine the remaining 1 cup cream, sour cream, confectioners' sugar, and vanilla in a large mixing bowl. Beat at medium speed to soft peaks.

5 To assemble, place an uncut pastry circle on serving plate and top with half the filling and half the peach slices. Layer with the second uncut pastry circle, then remaining filling and peaches. Place the 8 wedges at a slight angle atop filling. Sift confectioners' sugar on top and garnish with mint leaves. Makes 8 servings.

PER SERVING		DAILY GOAL
Calories	560	2,000 (F), 2,500 (M)
Total Fat	38 g	60 g or less (F), 70 g or less (M)
Saturated fat	21g	20 g or less (F), 23 g or less (M)
Cholesterol	110 mg	300 mg or less
Sodium	286 mg	2,400 mg or less
Carbohydrates	52 g	250 g or more
Protein	6 g	55 g to 90 g

PEACHY PECAN CRISP

Here's a summery fruit crisp that can be assembled ahead, then baked when guests come to call. Nectarines make a terrific filling, too.

Prep time: 25 minutes
Baking time: 25 to 30 minutes
○ *Degree of difficulty: easy*

5   **pounds peaches, peeled and sliced**
2   **to 3 tablespoons granulated sugar**
1   **tablespoon fresh lemon juice**
¾   **cup firmly packed brown sugar**
½   **cup all-purpose flour**
1   **teaspoon cinnamon**
6   **tablespoons butter *or* margarine, cut up**
¾   **cup rolled oats, uncooked**
¾   **cup chopped pecans, toasted**

1 Preheat oven to 375°F. Butter a 13x9-inch baking dish. Combine peaches, granulated sugar, and lemon juice in a large bowl. Spoon into the prepared dish. (Can be made ahead. Cover and refrigerate up to 4 hours.)

2 For pecan-oat topping, combine brown sugar, flour, and cinnamon in a large bowl. With a pastry blender or 2 knives, cut in butter until mixture resembles coarse crumbs. Stir in oats and pecans. (Can be made ahead. Cover and refrigerate up to 24 hours.) Sprinkle pecan-oat topping evenly over fruit. Bake 25 to 30 minutes or until fruit is bubbly. (If topping browns too quickly, cover loosely with foil.) Makes 12 servings.

PER SERVING		DAILY GOAL
Calories	260	2,000 (F), 2,500 (M)
Total Fat	11 g	60 g or less (F), 70 g or less (M)
Saturated fat	4 g	20 g or less (F), 23 g or less (M)
Cholesterol	16 mg	300 mg or less
Sodium	68 mg	2,400 mg or less
Carbohydrates	41 g	250 g or more
Protein	3 g	55 g to 90 g

PEACHY KEEN PEELING

To make peeling peaches a breeze, start with ripe, peak-season fruit. Then, heat a medium saucepan of water to boiling. Add peaches one at a time and cook 20 seconds. Immediately transfer to a bowl of cold water and peel off skin with a small sharp knife. (This method also works beautifully with nectarines.)

For a fast peach or nectarine dessert that's even better than eating the fruit plain, slice peeled fruit and sprinkle with confectioners' sugar. Add a splash of amaretto liqueur or peach schnapps. Let stand at room temperature 15 minutes before serving.

APPLE BAKLAVA

Prep time: 1 hour plus cooling
Baking time: 35 to 40 minutes
Degree of difficulty: moderate

- 6 **Golden Delicious apples**
- 6 **Granny Smith apples**
- 2 **tablespoons unsalted butter (no substitutions)**
- ½ **cup plus 6 tablespoons granulated sugar, divided**
- 1 **teaspoon cinnamon, divided**
- 2½ **cups walnuts, chopped**
- ½ **teaspoon grated lemon peel**
- 24 **sheets phyllo dough**
- ½ **cup unsalted butter, melted (no substitutions)**
- 2 **tablespoons plain dry bread crumbs**
- 2 **tablespoons honey**
  Whipped Cream *or* vanilla ice cream

1 For apple layer, peel and slice apples. Melt butter in a large Dutch oven over high heat. Add apples, 6 tablespoons of the sugar and ½ teaspoon of the cinnamon. Cook, stirring occasionally, until apples are tender and juices are evaporated, 15 to 20 minutes. Cool completely.

2 Preheat oven to 400°F. Meanwhile, for nut mixture, combine nuts, remaining ½ cup sugar, remaining ½ teaspoon cinnamon, and lemon peel in a small bowl.

3 With a sharp knife, trim phyllo sheets to 13x9-inch rectangles and keep covered with plastic wrap. Brush a metal 13x9-inch baking pan with some of the melted butter. Place 1 phyllo sheet in pan and brush lightly with butter (keep remaining phyllo covered). Layer 5 more phyllo sheets on top, brushing each with butter. Spread 2 cups nut mixture on top and repeat layering with 6 more phyllo sheets and butter. Spread apple mixture on top; repeat layering with 6 more phyllo sheets and butter. Sprinkle remaining nut mixture and bread crumbs on top. Layer with the 6 remaining phyllo sheets and butter.

4 With a sharp knife, cut lengthwise through pastry and filling into 1½-inch wide strips, then cut diagonally at 2-inch intervals to make diamonds. Bake 35 to 40 minutes or until golden. Drizzle honey over the top and bake 5 minutes more. Cool in pan on a wire rack. Serve warm or at room temperature with whipped cream or ice cream. Makes 12 servings.

PER SERVING		DAILY GOAL
Calories	515	2,000 (F), 2,500 (M)
Total Fat	26 g	60 g or less (F), 70 g or less (M)
Saturated fat	7 g	20 g or less (F), 23 g or less (M)
Cholesterol	26 mg	300 mg or less
Sodium	180 mg	2,400 mg or less
Carbohydrates	68 g	250 g or more
Protein	8 g	55 g to 90 g

PHYLLO FACTS

This crisp pastry loves fruit. Here are some hints for frazzle-free handling:

- Phyllo dough is also called strudel leaves. They can be used interchangeably.

- Phyllo dough is available in 16-ounce packages, fresh or frozen. If you buy frozen, follow the package directions for thawing and remove what you need. You can wrap unused phyllo tightly and refreeze, or it will keep in the refrigerator 10 days.

- Since phyllo is paper thin, it dries out quickly. Keep it covered at all times with plastic wrap, wax paper or a damp towel.

- Have everything ready before you begin to assemble your dessert, including the pastry brush, melted butter or vegetable oil.

APPLE-CRANBERRY NAPOLEONS

We've lightened up the classic custard-filled Napoleon with a rosy homemade applesauce layered between crisp phyllo sheets.

Prep time: 25 to 30 minutes
Baking time: 12 to 15 minutes
Degree of difficulty: moderate

½ **cup finely chopped toasted walnuts**
2 **tablespoons plain dry bread crumbs**
¾ **cup plus 2 tablespoons granulated sugar, divided**
5 **sheets phyllo dough**
⅓ **cup butter, melted (no substitutions)**
2 **tablespoons butter (no substitutions)**
3 **pounds Granny Smith apples, peeled and diced (8 cups)**
1 **cup fresh *or* frozen cranberries, coarsely chopped**
1 **teaspoon grated orange peel**
   Cinnamon-Vanilla Custard Sauce (recipe page 114)
   Fresh cranberries, for garnish

1 Preheat oven to 375°F. Grease 1 cookie sheet. Combine nuts, bread, crumbs, and 2 tablespoons of the sugar in small bowl. Place 1 phyllo sheet on prepared cookie sheet. (Keep remaining phyllo covered with plastic wrap.) Brush with some of melted butter and sprinkle evenly with 2 tablespoons nut mixture. Layer remaining phyllo neatly on top, brushing each layer with butter and sprinkling with nuts.

2 Using a ruler to measure, cut phyllo lengthwise into 6 even strips with a sharp knife. Cut each strip crosswise into 4 pieces to total 24 rectangles. Place on cookie sheet and bake 12 to 15 minutes until golden and crisp. Cool on the cookie sheet.

3 Meanwhile, for apple-cranberry filling, melt the 2 tablespoons butter in a large skillet over medium-high heat. Add apples and remaining ¾ cup sugar; cook, stirring until apples are tender, 10 to 15 minutes. Stir in cranberries and cook 2 minutes more. Stir in orange peel; set aside.

4 Place 8 rectangles on a serving tray or plates. Spread about ¼ cup filling neatly on each. Add a second layer of phyllo and ¼ cup more filling. Top with remaining phyllo. Serve with Cinnamon-Vanilla Custard and garnish with cranberries. Makes 8 servings.

PER SERVING

WITHOUT CUSTARD		DAILY GOAL
Calories	357	2,000 (F), 2,500 (M)
Total Fat	16 g	60 g or less (F), 70 g or less (M)
Saturated fat	7 g	20 g or less (F), 23 g or less (M)
Cholesterol	28 mg	300 mg or less
Sodium	180 mg	2,400 mg or less
Carbohydrates	54 g	250 g or more
Protein	2 g	55 g to 90 g

NOTES

137

SANTA FE FRUIT CORNUCOPIAS

In this unusual fruit dessert, strawberries and mangos spiked with tequila are spooned into wafer-thin cornmeal cookie cones.

Prep time: 15 minutes
Baking time: 8 to 10 minutes minutes per batch
⊖ *Degree of difficulty: moderate*

¼ **cup butter (no substitutions)**
⅔ **cup plus 2 tablespoons granulated sugar, divided**
3 **large egg whites**
½ **teaspoon grated orange peel**
¼ **cup all-purpose flour**
2 **tablespoons yellow cornmeal**
2 **tablespoons tequila**
1 **pint strawberries, quartered**
1 **mango, diced**
1 **tablespoon chopped fresh mint**
1 **cup sweetened whipped cream**

1 For cornucopias, preheat oven to 350°F. Generously coat 2 cookie sheets with vegetable cooking spray. Beat butter and ⅔ cup of the sugar in a large mixing bowl at medium speed until light and fluffy. Add egg whites 1 at a time, beating well after each addition, then add orange peel. Beat in flour and cornmeal just until smooth. Let stand 10 minutes.

2 Spoon scant ¼ cup batter onto a prepared cookie sheet and spread into a 6-inch circle, 2 cookies per sheet. Bake 8 to 10 minutes or until edges are golden. Cool on cookie sheet 30 seconds, then loosen 1 cookie at a time with a long, flexible metal spatula and invert onto clean surface. Immediately roll cookie into a cone shape and prop an end open with a small glass or cup until set. Repeat process with remaining batter.

3 For filling, stir the remaining 2 tablespoons sugar and tequila together in a large bowl until sugar is dissolved. Add strawberries, mango, and mint to blend.

4 Place one cornucopia on each of 8 dessert plates. Spoon filling evenly into openings and top with dollops of whipped cream. Makes 8 servings.

PER SERVING		DAILY GOAL
Calories	265	2,000 (F), 2,500 (M)
Total Fat	13 g	60 g or less (F), 70 g or less (M)
Saturated fat	7 g	20 g or less (F), 23 g or less (M)
Cholesterol	37 mg	300 mg or less
Sodium	88 mg	2,400 mg or less
Carbohydrates	33 g	250 g or more
Protein	3 g	55 g to 90 g

NOTES

SUMMER FRUITS WITH VANILLA YOGURT CHEESE

Here's a bit of indulgence without the guilt—your guests will never know this sweet and satiny cheese came from a container of yogurt!

Total prep time: 10 minutes plus draining and chilling

○ *Degree of difficulty: easy*

- 1 **container (16 ounces) low-fat** *or* **nonfat vanilla** *or* **plain yogurt**
- 1 **strip (3 inches) orange peel**
- 5 **cups assorted fruits (strawberries, blueberries, raspberries, sliced peaches and nectarines)**

1 For cheese, line a fine mesh sieve or colander with a clean kitchen towel or large coffee filter. Place over a large bowl. Spoon yogurt into colander; stir in orange peel. Cover and refrigerate 6 hours or overnight. Discard liquid in bowl and transfer cheese to a serving bowl. (Can be made ahead. Cover and refrigerate up to 1 week.)

2 Arrange fruit on individual serving plates. Serve each with a dollop of yogurt cheese. Makes 4 servings.

PER SERVING		DAILY GOAL
Calories	145	2,000 (F), 2,500 (M)
Total Fat	2 g	60 g or less (F), 70 g or less (M)
Saturated fat	0 g	20 g or less (F), 23 g or less (M)
Cholesterol	3 mg	300 mg or less
Sodium	42 mg	2,400 mg or less
Carbohydrates	27 g	250 g or more
Protein	6 g	55 g to 90 g

WINTER FRUIT COMPOTE WITH DRIED TART CHERRIES

Prep time: 30 minutes
Cooking time: 5 to 8 minutes

○ *Degree of difficulty: easy*

- 4 **navel oranges, rinsed**
- 2 **tablespoons sour cream**
- ½ **cup port wine**
- ⅓ **cup plus 1 tablespoon granulated sugar, divided**
- 1 **ripe Bosc pear, peeled, cored, and cut into eight slices**
- 1 **Golden Delicious apple, peeled, cored, and cut into eight slices**
- ¼ **cup dried tart cherries**
- 2 **cups thinly sliced fresh pineapple**
- ½ **cup heavy** *or* **whipping cream**

1 Grate ¼ teaspoon orange peel and combine with sour cream in a small bowl; set aside.

2 With a sharp paring knife, cut peel and white pith from oranges. Remove segments and squeeze juice from membranes. Strain juice into a small saucepan and reserve orange segments in a serving dish. Add port and ⅓ cup of the sugar to saucepan; cook, stirring, over medium heat until sugar is dissolved. Add pear, apple, and cherries. Simmer until tender, 5 to 8 minutes. Gently stir into oranges. Stir in pineapple slices.

3 Beat cream with remaining 1 tablespoon sugar in a large mixing bowl to stiff peaks. Fold in sour cream mixture. Serve compote with whipped cream. Makes 6 servings.

PER SERVING		DAILY GOAL
Calories	270	2,000 (F), 2,500 (M)
Total Fat	9 g	60 g or less (F), 70 g or less (M)
Saturated fat	5 g	20 g or less (F), 23 g or less (M)
Cholesterol	29 mg	300 mg or less
Sodium	14 mg	2,400 mg or less
Carbohydrates	45 g	250 g or more
Protein	2 g	55 g to 90 g

CLASSIC SUMMER PUDDING

This traditional English treat is made with good-quality bread soaked with the juices of fresh berries. Simple and satisfying, it's low in fat, too.

Prep time: 15 minutes plus chilling
Cooking time: 4 minutes
O *Degree of difficulty: easy*

8 to 9 slices firm white bread, crusts removed
5 cups assorted fresh berries (raspberries, blackberries, blueberries, and sliced strawberries)
½ cup granulated sugar
Low-fat plain *or* vanilla yogurt

1 Line a 1-quart bowl with bread, trimming edges to fit. Combine berries and sugar in medium saucepan. Heat, stirring, over medium heat just until sugar is dissolved and berries release their juice, about 4 minutes. Pour fruit and juice into bread-lined bowl. Top with a layer of bread and cover loosely with plastic wrap. Place on a plate and cover with a saucer that fits just inside the bowl. Weight down with a 2-pound can. Refrigerate overnight.

2 To serve, remove can, saucer, and plastic wrap. Run a knife around edge of bowl to loosen pudding. Invert onto plate. Cut into wedges and serve with a dollop of yogurt. Makes 6 servings.

PER SERVING
WITHOUT YOGURT   DAILY GOAL

Calories	210	2,000 (F), 2,500 (M)
Total Fat	1.5 g	60 g or less (F), 70 g or less (M)
Saturated fat	0 g	20 g or less (F), 23 g or less (M)
Cholesterol	1 mg	300 mg or less
Sodium	175 mg	2,400 mg or less
Carbohydrates	47 g	250 g or more
Protein	4 g	55 g to 90 g

BERRIED TREASURES

Savor the glorious fruits of summer all year. Simply freeze a supply of blueberries, raspberries, strawberries, or even cherries. Arrange fresh berries about ½ inch apart on cookie sheets, then freeze until berries are completely firm. Transfer frozen fruit to freezer-proof bags or containers. You can substitute unthawed berries for fresh in your favorite dessert recipe.

141

METRIC COOKING HINTS

By making a few conversions, cooks in Australia, Canada, and the United Kingdom can use the recipes in Ladies' Home Journal® *100 Great Dessert Recipes* with confidence. The charts on this page provide a guide for converting measurements from the U.S. customary system, which is used throughout this book, to the imperial and metric systems. There also is a conversion table for oven temperatures to accommodate the differences in oven calibrations.

Volume and Weight: Americans traditionally use cup measures for liquid and solid ingredients. The chart (top right) shows the approximate imperial and metric equivalents. If you are accustomed to weighing solid ingredients, here are some helpful approximate equivalents.
- 1 cup butter, castor sugar, or rice = 8 ounces = about 250 grams
- 1 cup flour = 4 ounces = about 125 grams
- 1 cup icing sugar = 5 ounces = about 150 grams

Spoon measures are used for smaller amounts of ingredients. Although the size of the tablespoon varies slightly among countries, for practical purposes and for recipes in this book, a straight substitution is all that's necessary.

Measurements made using cups or spoons should always be level, unless stated otherwise.

Product Differences: Most of the ingredients called for in the recipes in this book are available in English-speaking countries. However, some are known by different names. Here are some common American ingredients and their possible counterparts:
- Sugar is granulated or castor sugar.
- Powdered sugar is icing sugar.
- All-purpose flour is plain household flour or white flour. When self-rising flour is used in place of all-purpose flour in a recipe that calls for leavening, omit the leavening agent (baking soda or baking powder) and salt.
- Light corn syrup is golden syrup.
- Cornstarch is cornflour.
- Baking soda is bicarbonate of soda.
- Vanilla is vanilla essence.

USEFUL EQUIVALENTS

⅛ teaspoon = 0.5 ml
¼ teaspoon = 1 ml
½ teaspoon = 2 ml
1 teaspoon = 5 ml
¼ cup = 2 fluid ounces = 50 ml
⅓ cup = 3 fluid ounces = 75 ml
½ cup = 4 fluid ounces = 125 ml
⅔ cup = 5 fluid ounces = 150 ml
¾ cup = 6 fluid ounces = 175 ml
1 cup = 8 fluid ounces = 250 ml
2 cups = 1 pint
2 pints = 1 litre
½ inch = 1 centimetre
1 inch = 2 centimetres

BAKING PAN SIZES

American	Metric
8x1½-inch round baking pan	20x4-centimetre sandwich or cake tin
9x1½-inch round baking pan	23x3.5-centimetre sandwich or cake tin
11x7x1½-inch baking pan	28x18x4-centimetre baking pan
13x9x2-inch baking pan	32.5x23x5-centimetre baking pan
2-quart rectangular baking dish	30x19x5-centimetre baking pan
15x10x2-inch baking pan	38x25.5x2.5-centimetre baking pan (Swiss roll tin)
9-inch pie plate	22x4- or 23x4-centimetre pie plate
7- or 8-inch springform pan	18- or 20-centimetre springform or loose-bottom cake tin
9x5x3-inch loaf pan	23x13x6-centimetre or 2-pound narrow loaf pan or paté tin
1½-quart casserole	1.5-litre casserole
2-quart casserole	2-litre casserole

OVEN TEMPERATURE EQUIVALENTS

Fahrenheit Setting	Celsius Setting*	Gas Setting
300°F	150°C	Gas Mark 2
325°F	160°C	Gas Mark 3
350°F	180°C	Gas Mark 4
375°F	190°C	Gas Mark 5
400°F	200°C	Gas Mark 6
425°F	220°C	Gas Mark 7
450°F	230°C	Gas Mark 8
Broil		Grill

Electric and gas ovens may be calibrated using Celsius. However, increase the Celsius setting 10 to 20 degrees when cooking above 160°C with an electric oven. For convection or forced-air ovens (gas or electric), lower the temperature setting 10°C when cooking at all heat levels.